The Metaphysics
of the Social World

The Metaphysics
of the Social World

David-Hillel Ruben

Routledge & Kegan Paul
London, Boston, Melbourne and Henley

First published in 1985
by Routledge & Kegan Paul plc

14 Leicester Square, London WC2H 7PH, England

9 Park Street, Boston, Mass. 02108, USA

464 St Kilda Road, Melbourne,
Victoria 3004, Australia and

Broadway House, Newtown Road,
Henley on Thames, Oxon RG9 1EN, England

Set in Palatino
by Columns of Reading
and printed in Great Britain
by
T.J. Press (Padstow) Ltd.
Padstow, Cornwall

Library of Congress Cataloging in Publication Data

Ruben, David-Hillel.

The metaphysics of the social world.
Includes index.
1. Social sciences – Philosophy. 2. Social
sciences – Methodology. I. Title.
H61.R73 1985   301   84-18095

British Library CIP data also available

ISBN 0-7100-9826-X

For those who went before me
And for those who will come after me.
But especially for Anna, Sophie, and Simon
And for Eira, who alone goes with me.

Contents

	Preface and acknowledgments	ix
Chapter 1	The existence of social entities	1
Chapter 2	Social wholes and parts	45
Chapter 3	Social properties and their basis	83
	Appendix to chapter 3	128
Chapter 4	Methodological individualism	131
	First Appendix to chapter 4	173
	Second Appendix to chapter 4	177
	Notes	180
	Name Index	187
	Subject Index	188

Preface and Acknowledgments

This book is not intended to cover all or even many of the main philosophical issues and problems that are usually discussed in books about the philosophy of social science. Some readers may find the scope of this book excessively narrow, but I make no apologies for that. The book concentrates on a few, closely related problems in the philosophy of social science, and ignores the others almost entirely.

It is easy to state the main theses of the book: metaphysical individualism concerning social objects is false; social objects are not wholes whose parts are human individuals; social properties are not reducible to mental properties; methodological individualism, as a view about explanation in the social sciences, is false. What is perhaps surprising is that the entire book is concerned to develop and defend only these four theses, and even then, in some cases, I do not regard my own arguments as conclusive. It came as something of a surprise to me to find that I believe that these four theses are true. As in all significant questions of philosophy, I began thinking about these issues with intuitions pulling me to both sides of the questions. In the dispute between individualism and holism in the philosophy of social science, as in other metaphysical disputes, I felt myself torn between a healthy sense of material reality on the one hand, and a conflicting sense of the integrity of other areas of reality on the other. The more I thought about the problems, the more decisively in my own mind did the latter intuitions win out against the former.

I feel indebted to my two most recent past employers, the City University and the University of Essex. It may be that one gets or can get what they have given me from all universities; this I cannot say. But both have given me ample time for research, by creating a climate in which research and writing are taken seriously and encouraged.

I am especially indebted to R.M. Sainsbury, of King's College, London, for his patient discussion with me of too many philosophical problems to count. Had I not had him available for philosophical conversation, an essential condition for the development of my own thought would have been missing.

Finally I am grateful to *The Philosophical Quarterly* for permission to use material from my article, 'The existence of social entities', vol. 32, October 1982, no. 129, pp. 295-310; to *Mind*, for material from 'Social wholes and parts', vol. 92, April 1983, pp. 219-38; and to *Proceedings of the Aristotelian Society* for material from 'Social properties and their basis', vol. 85, new series, 1984-5, pp. 23-45.

David-Hillel Ruben
The London School of Economics
and Political Science

CHAPTER 1

The existence of social entities

In the debates about holism and individualism in the philosophy of the social sciences, a distinction is sometimes drawn between individualism as a metaphysical or ontological doctrine on the one hand, and as a thesis about laws or explanation on the other (the latter sometimes goes by the name 'methodological individualism'). Some writers have claimed that the purely metaphysical dispute, on its own, is not very interesting. For instance, J.W.N. Watkins says, 'If an answer to the question of social facts could throw light on the serious and interesting question of sociological laws, then the question of social facts would also be serious and interesting. But this is not so.'[1] I do not share Watkins's attitude. Suppose that there were social entities, which played no role whatever, or no irreducible role, in the explanation of events. This would still be of great philosophical interest, for it would tell us something about the nature and structure of reality, in spite of having no interest at all from the point of view of the methodology of the social sciences. I propose in this chapter, and in the two chapters that follow it, to consider this ontological question on its own, and to mark this, I speak of 'metaphysical' individualism or holism. What I say in these three chapters is consistent with a wide variety of views about how the methodological and metaphysical doctrines are related. It is

1

only in the fourth chapter of the book that I turn to a discussion of methodological individualism.

My discussion is metaphysical not only in the sense that contrasts with the methodological, but also in the sense that contrasts with the linguistic and epistemic. The metaphysical or ontological question is often couched in terms of the translatability of one discourse into another. Both Quinton and Mandelbaum pose the issue in this way: 'These are . . . ontological doctrines which can be expressed in the idiom of philosophical analysis as the theses that statements about social objects can or cannot be reduced, are or are not logically equivalent to, statements about individuals who are members of the groups or institutions in question';[2] 'My thesis that societal facts are irreducible to psychological facts may be reformulated as holding that sociological concepts cannot be translated into psychological ones without remainder.'[3] But surely this is an error. As David Armstrong pointed out in the context of a different ontological dispute,[4] it may be that there is no translation without remainder of physical object language into sense data language, or that one could not learn or explain the former solely on the basis of the latter, but for all that, physical objects just might be, *in rerum natura*, nothing but collections or sets of sense data. We might have two logically independent languages about one and the same order of things. Moreover, if we understand 'translatability of theory T_2 into theory T_1' as 'the derivability of T_2 from T_1 and bridge laws',[5] it is not at all clear that translatability insures that T_1 and T_2 are about the same sorts of objects. One might argue, for example, that mirror images remain as entities in their own right, in spite of the fact that all the truths about them can be derived from geometrical optics plus the necessary bridge laws. Like Armstrong's own discussion of sense data, I intend that the conclusion of the argument I will advance in this chapter be about the existence of an entity of a certain sort, rather than about our linguistic or epistemic abilities. Of course, where relevant, the premises of an argument with such an ontological conclusion might include premises about language, meaning, translation, learnability, or epistemic priority. However, I think we should be rightly suspicious of

2

any argument that claimed to demonstrate an ontological conclusion on the strength of such premisses alone. In the argument I will offer, there is a premiss about the *truth* of a certain belief, not just about its meaningfulness, and this is, of course, a different matter altogether.

I want to start by way of a distinction, standard enough in the general philosophical literature, but whose application in the philosophy of social science is not so common, namely the intuitive distinction between entities or objects on the one hand, and their properties, characteristics, or features on the other.[6] I call the distinction 'intuitive', because it is not my wish in this book to become involved in attempting a philosophically adequate characterisation of that distinction. Roughly, entities are what true statements or beliefs are about; properties are what statements ascribe to what they are supposed to be about. In this harmlessly wide sense, every predicate stands for a property. I do not say that the distinction is free from difficulty, but it will be sufficiently clear for the purposes of this book. I cannot see that deciding these controversial points one way rather than another will affect what I have to say.

Metaphysical individualism, then, can involve either of two distinct doctrines: (1) There are no irreducible social entities; (2) There are no irreducible social properties. In both (1) and (2), the word 'irreducible' is important, because metaphysical individualists might not wish to deny that Strathclyde County Council existed, or that there was such a property as that of being an alderman. Rather, they might say that neither case involved the existence of some irreducible social entity or property.

What is the relation between (1) and (2)? Clearly, they are consistent. Although my characterisation of the theses does not make it inconsistent to deny (1) and assert (2), the combination does not seem very attractive, for one would thereby be committed to the existence of irreducible social entities, all of whose properties were ultimately only individual ones, and it is hard to see what reasons we could have for belief that there were such entities. Just as an important motive for believing that there are mental or physical substances is the need for there to be bearers of mental or physical properties, so too an important reason for holding that there are social substances is the need for there to be bearers of a particularly interesting subset of social properties. I do not say that this is the only possible reason for believing that there are social substances, but certainly, in the absence of a belief in irreducible social properties, a major reason for crediting the existence of irreducible social substances is lost. I will return to this question in chapter 3.

Of more interest is the possibility of asserting (1) but denying (2), for it might be that the only sort of irreducible entities needed in social science are individuals, but that they can have irreducible social properties. This is what we appear to be asserting if we say that someone is an alderman, for example, because we refer only to an individual, but ascribe a social property to him. Thus, both (1) and (2), and (1) and not-(2), seem consistent, and offer two different versions of what might be called 'metaphysical individualism'. An entity individualist (an e-individualist), I shall say, holds (1) and may or may not hold (2); a property individualist (a p-individualist) holds (1) and (2).

There are, no doubt, numerous intuitions about reality that might prompt someone to call himself an individualist. It is obvious that there is some close relation between social entities and human individuals. If social entities exist, it cannot be just a contingent fact that some individuals or other do so as well. Attempts at characterising that relation might be in terms of whole and part, being made from, or being internally related to. However, as I understand the debate, the only relation available to the entity individualist is identity. The entity individualist holds that every allegedly social entity turns out to be identical with some non-social entity.

Anthony Quinton, in his paper to which I earlier referred, calls himself an individualist of sorts, on the grounds that societies are wholes whose parts are human individuals. Quinton also says that these social wholes are irreducible to the individuals who are their parts. I cannot see why this should count as any sort of individualism. Being the (proper) part of is a relation such that if it holds between a and b, a and b cannot be identical. Quinton believes that there are human individuals and that there are irreducible

4

social objects, and this seems as clear a statement of metaphysical holism as one could wish for.

In this chapter, the question on which I shall concentrate is whether there are any suitably individualistic entities with which reductively to identify social entities. I did not word (1) in terms of reductive identification of entities, for I wanted my characterisation of entity individualism to include the view which, despairing of any successful reductive identification, still claimed that there were no irreducible social entities at all, and therefore that our ordinary talk of them, far from being construable as being only about individual entities, was in fact about nothing whatever. In what follows, I discuss entity individualism only in the version that seeks a reductive identification of social entities to individual ones, although my wording of (1) takes into account the possibility of this alternative individualistic manoeuvre. I will return briefly to this possibility later in the chapter.

What is a reductive identification? On this large question, I wish to say the minimum necessary for my specific purposes in this book. I have in mind such paradigms of reductive identification as the attempts to identify physical objects with sets of sense data, selves with sets of experiences, numbers with sets of sets, mental states with brain states or dispositions to behaviour, moral properties with natural properties, the causal relation with universal regularity, and knowledge with justified true belief. Reminding ourselves of these other examples is not likely to inspire confidence of success in the case at hand; still, each attempt at reductive identification must be considered in its own terms, and that is what I propose to do here.

Suppose someone, offering one of these attempted reductive identifications, says that Fs are nothing but Gs. For example, he says that physical objects are nothing but sets of sense data. That is, for each physical object, there is some set of sense data with which it is identical. Further, a necessary if not sufficient condition for this is that for each physical object, there is some set of sense data necessary and sufficient for it. The force of 'necessary and sufficient' in this requirement is that one *cannot* have that physical object without having that set of sense data, and *cannot* have that set of sense data without having that physical object. The necessity and sufficiency must not be merely extensional, but necessary (either metaphysically or nomologically). The reductive identification of Fs with Gs is rebutted if it is possible for there to be an F but no G. It defeats the reductive identification of physical objects with sets of sense data if there could be, whether or not there ever actually is, a physical object but no set of sense data. (Indeed, it is for this reason that phenomenalists often talk in terms of actual *and possible* sets of sense data.) Similarly, it defeats the reductive identification of a mental state type with a brain state type if it can be shown that there is a physically possible world in which someone is in that type of mental state but not in that type of brain state, even if as a matter of fact the two do actually always go together. Extensional equivalence is too weak. It defeats the reductive identification of moral goodness with the natural property of maximising human happiness to show that it is possible for the first property to be true of a person but not the second, even if in fact this is never the case.

In what sense must such counterexamples be merely possible? In some cases, it is necessary to demonstrate nomologically possible counterinstances; in other cases, one need only meet the weaker requirement of demonstrating logically possible counterinstances. In those cases in which reductive identification is offered in the spirit of semantic analysis, it is only the latter, weaker, requirement that must be met. Plausible reductive identification of social with individual entities is offered in the spirit of philosophically inspired rational reconstruction rather than in the spirit of semantic analysis. It will be appropriate therefore to rebut such alleged identifications with nomologically possible counterinstances, rather than with merely logically possible ones. In any event, we are less likely to go amiss if we require of our rebuttal that it meet the stronger rather than the weaker of the two requirements.

What does it mean to say that an alleged reductive identification is circular? What we hope to achieve by a reductive identification is, literally, a reduction in ontic commitment. Suppose there is an allegedly reductive identification of Fs with Gs. Suppose further that someone can successfully argue that a necessary condition for there to be a G is that there is an F. If this claim can be sustained, then the reduction claim would have shown to be false, since commitment to Fs merely rearises in being committed to Gs. I am not saying that the identity claim will be shown to be false; it may be true. Fs might still *be* Gs, but the identity could not be reductive. We might call such a non-reductive identity claim 'circular'. An example might be this: suppose someone could successfully argue that a necessary condition for a person to have a justified belief s is that there is some piece of information r that the person has and he knows that r is a reason for thinking that s is true. If this were so, knowledge might still be justified true belief, but, since circular, this could not amount to a reductive identification of knowledge with justified true belief. Necessary co-extensiveness of Fs and Gs could itself be at best a necessary but insufficient condition for the *reductive* identification of Fs with Gs. A further condition that must be met is that of non-circularity.

To be more precise, in order to show that a claim to reductive identification fails on grounds of circularity, we must show that a necessary condition for the existence of a G is that there is an F, where that dependence does not simply arise from the truth of the identity claim itself. Suppose we know that Fs are Gs, but we do not know if the identity is reductive or circular. From the fact that Fs are Gs, we can infer that a necessary condition for the existence of a G is that there is an F, because this is itself part of what is entailed by saying that Fs and Gs are identical. If this alone were sufficient to establish circularity, then every identity claim would be circular, and this neither proponents nor opponents of reductive identity intended. Rather, what must be done to defeat on grounds of circularity a claim of reductive identity of Fs with Gs is to show that if there is a G, then there must be an F, *independently* of the identity claim itself.

We should note too the kind of circularity being alleged. One idea of circularity is that you end up with the specific

7

item with which you started. Another idea of circularity is that you end up with the same *sort* of thing with which you started. It is this second kind of circularity that I claim to find. The reductions we are considering, both here and in chapter 3, do not just aim at eliminating specific social entities or properties. They aim to show that the very categories of social entity or social property are ontologically redundant, since all such entities or properties are in reality nothing more than material or mental entities or properties. Therefore, in an identification of social entity s with (say) some mental entity m, in order to sustain the charge of circularity, I do not need to show that, in the further analysis of m, the entity s itself reappears. It is enough to show that, in the analysis of m, some social entity or other reappears (it may or may not be s). These remarks apply, *mutatis mutandis*, to my charge of circularity in chapter 3. Most anti-reductivist charges of circularity allege circularity of this second type. For example, in arguing that the analysis of 'x knows that p', in terms of justified true belief, is circular, one would not need to show that 'x knows that p' itself rearises in the analysis of what it is for a belief to be justified. It is sufficient, to sustain the circularity charge, to show (if one can) that *some* item of knowledge is required in the analysis of justified belief that p, but the item may not be knowledge that p.

Entity individualism

I want to turn to a discussion of social entities, whose existence is denied by the entity individualist. It is with the truth of (1) that I shall be concerned in this chapter. This chapter could at most be only half a treatment of meta-physical or ontological individualism, since I discuss in it only the question of social entities, not of social properties. I reserve the discussion of the latter until chapter 3.

I do not even deal here with all the sorts of social entities that might be said to exist. Social entities, if there are such things, might be thought to include particular *social substances* like France, Ealing, and the Red Cross; *social types* like capitalism, dictatorship, and bureaucracy; *events* like the assassination of Allende, the Great Crash of 1929, and the conversion of Clovis; *processes* like the decline of the Roman Empire, the accumulation of capital in western Europe in the nineteenth century, the disappearance of feudal relations in the towns in the late middle ages; *states* like servitude, industrial capacity, class antagonism, and the sexual division of labour. I do not intend my catalogue to beg any questions concerning the irreducible existence of any entities that fall under the categories mentioned. I offer the catalogue only as a reminder of the very different sorts of entities about which the holist and individualist may be arguing. No doubt my catalogue is itself contentious. Other categories of entities could be mentioned, or the ones I have offered disputed. There are also interesting questions about priority relations between the categories. I intend to sidestep all of this discussion by focusing on only one sort of (putative) entity, namely social substances. Social substances, like France, are particulars (unlike types, such as capitalism, which can have multiple exemplifications), and are the continuants to which various states, processes, and events can be ascribed. The entity individualism I wish to consider is a specific form of (1), namely (1'): There are no irreducible social substances. If (1') is false, then (1) is false. It is rather odd, when one comes to think about it, that, at least since the time of Weber, so much of the holist-individualist controversy has been conducted in terms of the reality or ideality of types. I want to shift this misplaced focus away from social types and onto social substances.

The argument stated

As I said, I will argue that (1') is false, and since if there are irreducible social substances, there must be irreducible social entities of at least one kind, (1) is false. My argument is this:

(1)   The belief that France is a charter member of the United Nations is literally true.

(2)   The belief in (1) seems to require the existence of France as that which the belief is about.

(3)   The belief in (1) is not paraphrasable by, or logically equivalent to, any belief that does not require the existence of France for its truth.

(4)   There are no acceptable candidates with which France may be reductively identified.

∴   (5)   There is at least one irreducible social substance, France.

The argument relies on the idea that our ordinary modes of thinking and speaking appear to carry ontological commitments, and, if we are to accept these thoughts or assertions as true, either we must accept the ontological commitments or we must give an account of our thinking and speaking which shows that these apparent commitments are not genuine ones. W.V.O. Quine formulates this idea explicitly, but it is not necessary to agree with the specific details of his position to appreciate the general view. What is to be avoided is 'such philosophical double talk, which would repudiate an ontology while enjoying its benefits. . .'.[7] Apparent ontological commitments in what we say or think are to be taken seriously, either to be accepted or to be shown to be merely apparent. It is this general idea that my argument uses, and applies to the way in which we think and speak of the social world, whether in social science itself or in our ordinary, pre-scientific discourse.

Although I think that my argument is sound, there are at least three ways in which I fail to demonstrate its soundness. The first way concerns premiss (4). I will run through various reductive possibilities for the entity which the belief in (1) is about. I dismiss them in turn. No strategy of this sort could rule out the possibility that there is some unconsidered candidate that fits the bill, but I discuss the possibilities most frequently mentioned in the literature, and therefore I believe that I render the acceptance of (4) rational.

The second way in which I fail to demonstrate the

soundness of my argument concerns (1). As I mentioned earlier when I spoke of an alternative manoeuvre available to the individualist, a convinced entity individualist, persuaded of the truth of (2), (3), and (4), but equally sure on general metaphysical or other grounds of the falsity of the conclusion, might decide to abandon (1). He may come to accept that our talk about society *is* shot through with irreducible ontological commitments that he regards as intolerable. His position might be something like Hume's, according to one standard interpretation, on the continued and independent existence of objects. Our talk about France might be literal falsehood, since such talk assumes that a social substance exists, and this he will regard as false. He might be willing to concede that there are heuristic reasons for talking, and continuing to talk, in these ways. Indeed, he might even believe that it is a natural fact about ourselves that we must think of the world as containing these social entities. But whether such talk is useful or even necessary, it will be, on his view, simply false.

Such an individualist will then offer individual entities, as Hume offered impressions, not as reductive identifiers for problematic entities, but as all that can be saved in the way of literal truth from the way in which we ordinarily think or conceive of things. Individual entities would be thought of as replacements for rather than reducers of social entities. I have in mind here the distinction between reduction and elimination, as it is sometimes applied to distinguish varieties of materialism.[8] Reductive materialism accepts that there are sensations, for example, but that each sensation is identical with something material. Eliminative materialism asserts that there are no sensations. Analogously, one can distinguish between reductive and eliminative individualism, as a metaphysical thesis about social reality. In this chapter, my argument really only confronts reductive individualism, which accepts that there are nations, societies, associations – because beliefs like the one mentioned in (1) can be true – but identifies each such thing with some individual entity.

What of eliminative individualism? It asserts that, literally, there are no nations, societies, associations, and so on,

11

although it might concede some heuristic or other value to these beliefs. I think that it will be granted that eliminative individualism, like eliminative materialism, has a far smaller initial plausibility than does its reductive analogue. The sorts of considerations sufficient to get us to treat our talk of social items as false would have to be very compelling indeed. What we should demand of any such eliminative position is an answer to the question: what are the general metaphysical or epistemological grounds that make such an individualist sufficiently sure of the falsity of some conclusion like (5) to abandon the (apparent) truth of some belief like (1)?

Often enough, as in the case of Hume on the continued and independent existence of objects, the reason will be epistemological; that such entities could not be the objects of human knowledge. I do not think that the chances of any such argument being sufficiently strong to convince us to abandon our pre-theoretic beliefs about social substances like France are very good. Quinton, for instance, argues that 'social objects cannot be observed'.[9] In the next paragraph, he says that relatively small ones, like the British Cabinet, are 'straightforwardly observable'. By the end of that same paragraph, the claim has become that 'social objects are not, on the whole, effectively observed', because they are too large and scattered. What Quinton seems to assume in this weakened thesis is that to observe x 'effectively', I must observe every bit of x, an assumption which will render physical objects effectively unobserved, since I only see their surfaces, or some of their sides but not others. All of the epistemological arguments that I am aware of, which might be supposed to show that the belief in irreducible social substances must be false or unjustifiable, are similarly unconvincing. Although I do not demonstrate that premiss (1) is true, I think it is reasonable to assume that beliefs like the one mentioned in (1) are sometimes literally true, even if reduction of social substances were to fail.

The third way in which I fail to demonstrate the soundness of my argument concerns (3). The reason that I do not deal with this point here in any depth is that it concerns questions of language, and these are the questions

I have eschewed in favour of general metaphysics. It is important to add, though, that I have chosen my example to be about France, partly with this issue in mind. If one were to choose as the sample belief, as is sometimes done in the literature, the belief that the average family has 3.2 members, it is child's play to show that this involves us in no unwanted existential commitment to an average family (because this belief is logically equivalent to one in which 'the average family' does not occur). An example of Quinton's is 'The French middle class is thrifty', which he says is equivalent to 'Most French middle-class people are thrifty'. J.W.N. Watkins says that the belief that the Jewish race is cohesive is merely the belief that 'Jews usually marry Jews, etc.'.[10] But no such translation or equivalence is available for the example that I have chosen. There does not even seem to be a candidate assertion that suggests itself as logically equivalent to 'France is a charter member of the United Nations', and in which 'France' does not occur.

Premiss (4): The first candidate for reduction

What I shall therefore be concerned with in the remainder of my discussion of entity individualism is the truth of (4). I shall discuss several candidates for the reducing entity in the reductive identification of France with some individual entity. One such reductive candidate that I should like to dismiss quite quickly is the one that takes 'France' to be the name of a geographical portion of the earth's surface, in the way in which 'Polynesia', 'the Middle East', and 'Africa' are names of certain physical expanses.

Russell claimed that we 'can define "France" by its geographical boundaries'.[11] I do not say that we never do use 'France' in this way, but only that sometimes we do not, and in that sense it can be true to say that a nation like France might cease to exist (suppose it were absorbed by Italy), without any portion of the earth's surface ceasing to exist. Because 'Asia', 'Polynesia', and so on are only names of portions of the earth's surface, they (unlike France) are not the names of social substances. If Polynesia ceased to exist, some part of the earth's land mass would vanish, but if France ceased to exist, there may be no change in the earth's land mass whatever. Although Russell may have identified *a* use of 'France', he cannot have identified its only use.

So little can a social substance be identified with the physical space that it occupies that two distinct social substances can occupy one and the same space. Suppose for example that English County Councils had exactly the same physical boundaries as Church of England dioceses, and hence that every such council occupied precisely the same space as some diocese. All the same, no council and diocese would be identical. I conclude that social substances, like France, cannot be identified with the spatial area they inhabit. Not all social substances are even occupiers of space – e.g., the Red Cross does not have any obvious physical location, although its headquarters does. But when a social substance does occupy space, like France, it is necessarily located in some space, yet there is no exact space in which it is necessarily located. France can change its frontiers, and hence the area it occupies, at least to some extent; no physically defined area of land can alter its position and yet preserve its numerical identity. France, therefore, cannot be identical with any geographical portion of the earth's surface.

All that I need for my argument above is the contention that there is no exact space in which France is necessarily located; in other words, I assert that some spatial changes are identity-preserving for France. In fact, I believe something much stronger than that: there is no space at all in which France is necessarily located. That is, I believe that there is no spatial change of location which is logically inconsistent with the numerical identity of France. It may be difficult to imagine France not being located where Paris or Lyons or Poitiers now are, indeed to imagine France occupying the space now occupied by Greece. But these difficulties arise from contingent beliefs about the likely future course of change and development. The Mongols, Huns, Ostrogoths and Jews are examples of nations, or peoples, whose occupancy of space was radically transformed in the course of history. Of course, I do not intend merely to say that the French could all live in Greece, but that France could have this location too. To make this plausible, one could tell a story in which there was a gradual shift of location over a long period of time, so that at the end of the territorial transformation, France occupied the physical area now occupied by Greece. France would then occupy a location which did not even share a proper part with its original location. I cannot see that such a view contains any inconsistency or logical impossibility.

Premiss (4): The extensional candidate for reduction

What about more plausible reductive possibilities? Suppose we begin by trying to identify France with certain individuals. Sometimes one hears the slogan: 'Nations just are the individuals who make them up.' One of the several things wrong with this slogan is that, since 'individuals' is not a denoting or naming expression, there can be nothing it denotes or names. Since the reductive identification of France is committed to there being an entity with which France can be identified, the first task is to get clear what entity the slogan is casting for this role. Obviously, no individualist believes that France is identical with some particular individual, but what he might think is that France can be identified with the set of French persons, or the aggregate of them, or the group of French persons. These suggestions give us an entity, in a way which the slogan, which merely used the expression 'the individuals', did not give us.

The suggestions divide into extensional and non-extensional entities, in the following sense. Sets are extensional, since if a and b are sets, $a = b$ iff a and b have exactly the same members. Physical aggregates are extensional since if a and b are aggregates, $a = b$ iff a and b have exactly the same bits or constituents. Groups are non-extensional, because two non-identical groups can have precisely the same members, and because some changes in membership

15

are identity-preserving for a group. For example, two committees can have the same members, and a committee can retain numerical identity in spite of some changes in the membership of that committee. With groups, identity is not given by membership, but, *inter alia*, by the property or feature that individuals must possess in order to be rightly counted members of that group. My argument against reductive identification will be different for the two sorts of entities. It is often unclear whether an individualist has an extensional or non-extensional entity in mind as the candidate reductive identifier for social entities. For instance, Lessnoff says that 'Our analysis thus far has reduced social groups to individuals and systems of rules'.[12] 'Individuals and systems of rules' does not denote anything. Shall we interpret Lessnoff as identifying social groups with extensional sets which themselves contain extensional sets of individuals and non-extensional systems of rules, or with some non-extensional entity? This is, it seems to me, the first thing we must be clear about in evaluating any individualist proposal for reductive identification.

First, what is the case against sets, or aggregates, or indeed against the identification of France with any extensional entity? The argument I will now offer turns on no feature peculiar to social substances, for precisely the same argument will work against the reductive identification of a physical object with the set or aggregate of its material parts. I return to this distinction and its application to the case of ordinary material objects in chapter 2.

A reductivist might begin by saying that France can be reductively identified with the set of French persons. A holist objector might then point out that France cannot be identical with any set, since the identity conditions for sets and for France (and for social substances generally) are different. A set changes its identity if one member changes, yet nations, tribes, empires, associations and so on can retain numerical identity in the face of births and deaths of individual members or citizens.

But this rejoinder, as it stands, is too swift. Consider the set of all the French persons that there ever were, are, or will be (call this set '*a*'). Suppose the individualist claims that

France is identical with the set a. Never mind that we may now be in no position to say fully who all the members of the set are. I have eschewed all such points that relate to our epistemic or other abilities. Perhaps, metaphysically speaking, France just is that set of persons. What barrier could there be to this reductive identification, since there is no variation of members that in fact will ever occur that will change the identity of this set while leaving the numerical identity of France untouched? No individual will be born or die such that the identity of set a will be lost while France continues numerically the same, since the individualist will have taken into account all such actual changes in advance in his choice of sets.

The remaining barrier to the reductive identification concerns our modal and counterfactual beliefs about social substances. Regardless of whatever French persons there ever will be, France could have had one national more or less than it does have. If France had had this addition or loss to its citizenry, it might have remained numerically the same. But the set a could not have had one member more or less and still have remained the same set. So France cannot be identified with any set, or indeed with any other extensional entity, because they will differ at least in their modal or counterfactual properties.

Might not the individualist offer an alternative construal of our counterfactual beliefs about France, which will block the argument I have just given? What is uncontroversial is that we regard as true some of our beliefs of the form, 'France might have had one national more or less than it does have'. It does not follow however that we are forced to construe such beliefs as ascribing a counterfactual property to France. If France had this counterfactual property, then it could not be identical with any set, since no set can have such a property. But if we deny that the belief ascribes any counterfactual property to France, then the argument fails. Could we construe the belief in this way: 'There could have been, but is not, a set, b, which would have had the same members as the set a has, except that it had one member more or less'?. In other words, we might be able to understand the belief that France might have had one

17

national more or less not as falsely ascribing a counterfactual property to a set, but as making a true counterfactual claim about the existence of sets.

This will not do, and the reason is best brought out by considering not the general counterfactual belief about France, that it might have had one national more or less, but by considering the belief about France that some particular person might have been a national of it. Suppose that Bismarck's mother was in France just prior to his birth, but left for Prussia only moments before he was born (suppose he was born on a train just on the other side of the frontier). It would be true to say in such circumstances that Bismarck might have been a national of France if only his mother had delayed her departure by a few minutes. How might we construe this as a counterfactual claim about the existence of sets, and thus avoid the falsehood that the set a might have had an additional member? The suggestion we are considering would construe the belief that Bismarck might have been a national of France thus: 'There might have been but is not a set, b, just like set a, except that Bismarck would have been a member of set b'.

The difficulty here is that such a set b does actually exist, the set of French persons and Bismarck. It does not matter, of course, that we have no neat name for this set, for this is irrelevant to the question of its existence. This set b, the set of all the French persons and Bismarck, undoubtedly exists, so the counterfactual belief that there might have been *but is not* a set just like set a except that Bismarck was a member of it is false. Since it is false, it cannot serve as the construal of the true belief (according to my little story) that Bismarck might have been a national of France. I submit that this difficulty, the failure of sets to have the counterfactual properties that social substances can have, or the failure for there to be counterfactual facts about sets which might be the analogues of the counterfactual properties of social substances, bars the identification of social substances with sets or with any extensional entities whatever.

We might feel that the set b, the set of French persons and Bismarck, is irrelevant, because Bismarck does not belong to it in virtue of his being a French person. What the individualist might wish to say is this: 'There might have been, but is not, a set, namely the set of all French persons and Bismarck *qua* French.' This thought, although perfectly correct, moves away from the reductive identification of France with any extensional entity, because it makes the property under which the particulars are collected an essential property of the collection, in a sense which I wish now to explain.

Premiss (4): Non-extensional candidates for reduction

Let us call this kind of non-extensional entity a 'group'. I think that we do sometimes use that word in this way, or very close to this way, but if anyone is inclined to dispute this, let it be for him a technically defined term of art. I disregard the use of 'group' in mathematics for example, and restrict myself to those uses in which we speak of groups of persons.

Groups differ from sets in at least these two ways. First, groups can survive changes in membership; sets cannot. No change in membership is identity-preserving for sets, but some such changes are identity-preserving for groups.

Second, if sets a and b have the same members, then set a = set b, but this implication does not hold for groups. This is evidenced by the fact, as I have already mentioned, that two numerically distinct groups can have precisely the same members. It is also evidenced by some counterfactual truths about the members of sets that are not truths about members of groups. One truth is this: of the set of French persons, the members of that set could have been members of that very same set and not been French. But it is false of the group of French persons that they could have been members of the very same group and not have been French.

Intuitions to the contrary concerning this counterfactual truth about sets rests on a confusion between names and descriptions of sets. Consider the actual situation, in which the set a is the set of French persons, and is composed of individuals $a_1 \ldots a_n$. Compare this actual situation with a merely possible situation in which there are no French persons at all (France does not exist) and in which individuals $a_1 \ldots a_n$ are Ruritanian. The set a exists in both the actual and merely possible situations, because individuals $a_1 \ldots a_n$ do, and hence the set of them does, although the description, 'the set of French persons', true of set a in the actual world, describes or denotes only the empty set in the merely possible one.

Thus, it is true of the set a, which is in fact the set of all French persons, that its members could have been members of it even if they had not been French. But the same cannot be said for the group of French persons. Compare the actual situation in which there is a group of French persons composed of individuals $a_1 \ldots a_n$, with a merely possible situation in which there are no French persons at all but $a_1 \ldots a_n$ are Ruritanian. There is no group which exists in both the actual and merely possible situation, because there is no group of Ruritanians in the actual situation and no group of French in the merely possible situation. So, if France had never existed, the individuals could not have been members of the group of French persons. The individuals $a_1 \ldots a_n$ might still have existed, but 'collecting' the same individuals under a different property, 'Ruritanian', rather than 'French', changes group identity in a way in which set identity is not impaired.

Groups survive the rebuttal that we have given to the idea that social substances could be reductively identified with sets. The set of French persons and Bismarck exists, so there seems no way to capture with sets the counterfactual belief that Bismarck might have been French. But there does not exist a (national) group that includes all the French people and Bismarck, because there is no property of being some specific nationality that collects them – although of course there could have been.

Could France be reductively identified with some non-extensional entity, for instance with some group in my sense? Before I answer this, I want to say something more about groups, in the non-extensional sense I have indicated and in which human beings are the sorts of things that belong to them.

There is an intuitively acceptable sense, I think, in which the French constitute a distinct and identifiable group. So too do the unemployed, white-collar workers, and the Plymouth Brethren. Is there a group whenever there is a corresponding set of individuals? For example, there is certainly a set of buck-toothed individuals; is there a group of buck-toothed individuals? As far as I know, there is no such group, although there could have been. In general, there could have been a group of individuals 'collected' by almost any property: the property of being left-handed, of having buck teeth, of living north of the Iberian peninsular. In these three cases, there are in fact no such groups, because there is no general practice, no rule-in-use, by which people are singled out in a socially significant manner by these properties. I shall have more to say in chapter 3 about what this means, but it is sufficient here merely to claim that this is in fact how we do regard the existence of groups. So groups exist only when individuals with some common property are regarded, or regard themselves, in certain socially significant ways, whereas of course sets of individuals exist quite apart from these further considerations. I shall speak of a property as 'a collecting property' not just when it is true of some individuals, but only when it is used in a socially significant way to designate those individuals. A parallel might be found with H.L.A. Hart's conception of a rule of recognition.[13] The rule of recognition specifies the criterion according to which some first-order rule counts as a valid law of the realm. An example might be that anything approved by the Queen in Parliament is a valid law. Hart says that the rule of recognition exists in the practices of at least the officials, if not the general populace. That is, the rule of recognition is a practice, or rule-in-use, according to which a property is specified, like being approved by the Queen in Parliament, possession of which qualifies a first-order rule as valid law. Similarly, a collecting property is one that is actually in use in a socially significant way to distinguish some persons from others, and hence as constituting an identifiable group.

One might, to be sure, speak of possible groups in the absence of these further considerations about socially

21

significant use, for example the possible group of persons with buck teeth. But this is only to say that although there could have been such a group, in fact there is not.

The concept of a group, like the concept of a (public) rule-in-use or a practice, seems not only to be a non-extensional notion, but also an intrinsically social one. Groups exist, as I have stressed, not just in virtue of there being individuals who share a common property, but in virtue of their being so singled out in a socially significant manner. The qualification, 'socially significant manner', is important and cannot be omitted. In speaking of the set of individuals who have buck teeth, I have certainly singled out individuals who possess a common property. But I have not brought it about that such a group exists. In order for that to occur, either they would have to band together and constitute themselves as a group, or we would have to come to think of them as a group for some social purposes (discrimination in job applications, recipients of special dental treatment, or whatever). Because of this, to identify France with some group could not be to avoid the postulation of any social entity whatever, for a group just is a certain kind of social entity. To identify France with a group could not be reductive of all commitment to social entities, since groups are as social as nations. Lessnoff, it will be recalled, claimed the reduction of social groups to individuals and systems of rules. I have already argued that social groups cannot be identified with sets of individuals, etc. Now, it might be claimed that there are non-extensional entities other than groups which, unlike groups, are also not social, and with which France, and perhaps even social groups, can be reductively identified. I cannot claim to have demonstrated the truth of premiss (4), in part because I cannot demonstrate that there are no such non-extensional but also non-social candidates for the reduction. But I cannot think of any plausible candidates meeting this requirement. The choice seems to be between extensional sets or aggregates on the one hand and non-extensional but social groups on the other. If so, if Lessnoff is to avoid sets of individuals, he must be construed as identifying social groups with social groups, and although this identification has the merit of being undoubtedly true, no one could possibly think it was reductive of any ontological commitments.

On the other hand, there might be a significant advantage in identifying France, and similar examples of social substances, with some group of individuals, even if the advantage could not be a reductive advantage. For example, one might plausibly claim to have 'illuminated' the concept of a law of nature by the idea of a universal generalisation inductively supportable by its instances, without claiming that any genuine reduction in ontic or conceptual commitment had been achieved. Whether this is so depends on whether the concept or idea that is said to do the illuminating is really more perspicuous or comprehensible than the one that is said to be getting illuminated. In spite of the fact that the idea of a group is itself a social concept, groups may seem more readily understandable entities than nations, and so it might be thought that the former can shed non-reductive light on the latter. Whether this thought can be sustained depends in part, I think, on the selection of the group that is to do the illuminating.

In what follows, I do not return to the point that the concept of a group is itself social. My reason for this is as follows. Suppose that I am wrong and that 'group', in its non-extensional sense in which persons belong to them, can be given a non-social explication. In that case, I would still wish to give independent reasons for thinking that social substances like France could not be reductively identified with any group. Of course, I make no pretence of having considered and dismissed every possible group, but I do consider and dismiss three obvious candidates. For this reason too, I cannot say that I have demonstrated the truth of premiss (4), but I cannot think of any plausible groups that I fail to consider as reductive identifiers for France.

Of the three groups that I consider, the first could not be identified with France at all. The second and third groups are such that their existence presupposes the existence of France, so even if they could be identified with France, they could not be reductively identified with France. Finally, the second and third groups are not only incapable of serving as reductive identifiers for France. They are even incapable of providing any non-reductive illumination of what it is for France to exist, since they so immediately presuppose France's existence themselves. To put the matter rather baldly, in the case of non-reductive explications which are still meant to illuminate, one will have to tolerate large circles. There may be a family of interrelated ideas and concepts, such that every idea in the family presupposes others, but if the families are large enough, one may be able to use one idea or notion to shed light on another idea which is sufficiently distant from it in the circle so that their interrelations are mediate and non-obvious. But small families are intolerable for these purposes. It cannot be illuminating to explain necessary truth as what is true in all logically possible worlds, although one might offer this remark not in the spirit of illumination but rather merely to indicate which of two ideas one has decided to treat as basic relative to the other. Similarly, in the case of the last two groups I consider, they could not even provide a non-reductive but illuminating explication of France's existence, because the family of notions that are mutually implicated is too small to permit any illumination of one by the other. Their relations are immediate and obvious.

Premiss (4): The first candidate

Groups are identified by their collecting properties, and of the three groups I consider, one uses a social collecting property, one a psychological collecting property, and one a natural or physical collecting property. In this way, each group is an example of a large class of groups with either other physical, or other social, or other psychological collecting properties, so that in discussing these particular examples, I hope that some wider applications can be made. If there are some non-extensional entities other than groups, my arguments in what follows will apply to them, if they must use similar collecting properties to the ones I discuss.

The first candidate I want to discuss is the group of persons who share some particular physical property, let us say the property of being the biological descendants of some individual, or having some blood type. It seems to me obvious that no group of persons sharing any natural or physical property could be reductively identified with France. It is possible that there be social groups with a purely physical or biological collecting property, although as a matter of fact it is much harder to find any real examples of this than one might suppose (Chinese but not Japanese are 'coloureds' in South Africa, Indians but not Turks are 'blacks' in Britain – both examples suggest that the criteria for membership in these social groups are partly social). What I am claiming is that no such group, whether social or not, could be what France is identical with. Suppose some individualist claimed that France was identical with some group of persons with a certain blood type, or who are the biological descendants of some individual, or have a certain physical appearance. We know that nothing like this could be adequate, because the criteria for being French are legal. Even if all the persons accounted French by the legal criteria were as a matter of fact descended from some one person, or had some distinctive blood type, this would only be an accidental connection. We know that someone *could* be French even if descended from someone else or with a different blood type. The biological or physical property will not give us the right answer for possible cases, even if it gave us, coincidentally, the right answer in all actual cases, and that is sufficient to defeat the reductive identification.

In one sense, the coincidence of the biological and legal properties might not be just accidental. It is highly improbable, but not impossible, that there be a principle of French law which stated that the possession of some physical or biological property was necessary and sufficient for being French. But the point to emphasise in this sort of case is that the person would not be French just in virtue of having that property, but because that property was designated necessary and sufficient by French law. And French law can always change. That would be to say that even in this sort of case there would be possible if not actual examples in which people were French in spite of the fact that they failed to possess those physical or biological characteristics, and this fact is again sufficient to defeat the attempted reductive identification of France with some group of persons who possess any purely physical or biological property.

Premiss (4): The second non-extensional candidate

The first of the two rather more serious candidates for the role of collecting property, in the attempted reductive identification of France with the group of persons satisfying that property, is naturally suggested by my remarks about the first candidate. France cannot be identified with the group of persons with some physical property, because there could (in the weaker than logical sense) be French persons who failed to have that physical property. Why not then identify France simply with the group of persons who are French? Why not let the property of being French be the relevant collecting property?

The difficulty with this suggestion is that this property, being French, and the analogous property for other groups (e.g. being an Apache, a Roman, a member of the Association of University Teachers, a Red Cross worker), are implicitly relational. Being a Red Cross worker and being French are dyadic relations, with one term of the relation already specified. Being a Red Cross worker is to be understood as being a worker for the Red Cross, and being French as being a national of France. These relations seem to hold between persons and social substances. There does not appear to be any possibility of reductive identification, since the second terms of these relations appear to be social substances.

I have asserted that the property of being a French person is a relational property. I do not suppose that anyone will doubt that 'being French' and 'being a national of France' are two names for the same property. It is not obvious what should be made of this fact. I have said that, on inspection, the apparently non-relational property, being French, turns out to be the relational property, being a national of France. Suppose the individualist claims that what my argument really shows is that the apparent relation, being a national of

France, turns out, on inspection, to be the non-relational property, being French. If 'being French' and 'being a national of France' are two names for the same property, then either 'being French' is the name of a relation, or 'being a national of France' is, despite appearances, the name of a non-relational property. I have assumed the former, but how do we know that it is not the latter alternative that is true, especially since it would seem to have Occam's razor in its favour?

I argue that 'being French' and 'being a national of France' are two names for a relational property. The test for whether a property is relational is this. A property P is non-relational iff it is logically possible for there to be a universe in which there is some object o, and o is P, and no other object exists. Of course, the property P can be relational in spite of the fact that only one thing is P. The test says that a property P cannot be relational if there can be something that is P and there be nothing else whatever. By this test, properties like being a brother and being a cause are correctly shown to be relational, since it is impossible for there to be a universe in which there is only one object and it be a cause or a brother. Of course, there can be a two-personed universe such that only one of them is a brother (for the other person is his sister), and perhaps a two-event universe with only one event a cause, since it could cause the second event but itself have no cause, and the second event be the cause of no further event.

It is important to require for the non-relationality of P only that it is possible for there to be a *single* object o that can be P and no other object exist, rather than it be possible that *every* object that is P can be P without another object existing. This last requirement would be inappropriate, because it would conflate the case in which relationality arose from the property with the case in which relationality arose from the objects themselves. That is, suppose there were two objects, a and b, such that the existence of each logically required the existence of the other. Even if P were non-relational, if a could be P, then it is impossible that there be a universe in which a is P and no other object exists, because it is impossible that there be a universe in which a exists and no other object. If P is non-relational, then it needs only to be possible that there be some one object which is P and no other object exist, and meeting this last requirement will insure that the property P is not relational, in spite of the fact that in some other cases P might be possessed by relational objects, i.e. objects whose existence logically requires the existence of some other object. Not all readers will accept the idea of relational objects as well as that of relational properties; for them, the distinction in this paragraph will prove unnecessary.

A great deal of philosophical controversy can be expressed as a disagreement about whether certain properties are or are not relational. For example, there is the phenomenalists' attempt at translation of physical object statements into statements about sense data, which seeks to construe 'being P' as 'appearing P to a normal observer', where 'P' stands for any sensible quality of an object. Other examples include the question of whether the property of understanding a language is relational or whether it could be the atttribute of a single person, whether psychological states such as belief and understanding relate individuals to propositions or other abstract objects, and whether the ascription of a property to an object involves a relation between the object and a universal.

No social property whatever is non-relational. A description of the criteria for a property's being social will make this clear, and I discuss these criteria in chapter 3. At this point, though, I ask the reader merely to examine his intuitions about the case at hand, using the test that I have indicated. Is it logically possible for there to be a universe in which there is a single person who is French and no other thing whatever exist? There could be, let us say, a universe in which there was a sole person and nothing else existed (he might be a disembodied mind). There could be a universe in which there were many persons, and only one of whom was French, for there seems nothing impossible about the idea of nationality status that as a matter of fact applied only to one person. But what there could not be is a universe in which there was a sole French person and nothing else whatever existed. The point is not epistemic; it is not that we, contemplating such a universe, would find it hard or impossible to tell if he were French rather than Dutch, or rather than stateless. Supposing a universe whose sole denizen was French would be as impossible as supposing a universe in which there was but a single object and it was a cause or a brother.

My argument shows that 'being French' is the name of a relational property, another name for which is 'being a national of France'. Certainly, *prima facie* the relation relates persons and France. The identification of France with the group of persons who are French has every appearance of being circular within a very small family of concepts indeed, since the property of being French seems to presuppose immediately and directly the existence of France.

My argument here has only been that the property of being French is a relational property, and that it *appears* to relate persons and France. An individualist may still wish to argue that what the relational property really does is only relate persons to persons. My argument here does not address this point at all; indeed, it is only this first chapter as a whole which is intended to have the force of blocking that move. The point is that he who wishes to make that move still has all his reductive work cut out for him. Identifying France with the group of persons who are French will not help the reductivist with that work, since once we realise that the property of being French is relational, and appears to relate persons to France, commitment to France seems to rearise in the commitment to the very entity which was supposed to reduce it.

I detect more generally a certain blindness in the literature to the problem of relationality in the analysis of social concepts or entities. Often, an author, writing in a reductivist spirit, asserts that a certain social event or entity is merely such-and-such, where 'such-and-such' appears to name or contain the name of a relation, one of whose relata appears to be a social event or entity. An example of this is Papineau's claim that 'inflation is simply people being able to get less goods in exchange for a given monetary unit'.[14] Papineau does not succeed in reducing commitment to the social in his analysis of a social process, inflation. What inflation gets identified with is the process or event(s) of people getting less goods for their money, and this seems to involve a triadic relation, true of people, goods (not themselves to be identified with material things), and monetary units (whatever they are). I do not assert that these are ineliminably social entities, but rather that one is simply unsure what has happened here, and whether or not there has been any gain, in terms of either reduction or even just illumination of what inflation is.

Premiss (4): The third non-extensional candidate

The third and final candidate for the role of what I have called the collecting property in the attempted reductive identification, or even just perspicuous identification, of France with the group of persons having that property, is the property of having certain specific beliefs or attitudes. I think that a quite standard line of individualist thought is that the reality that underlies our belief in the existence of things like France is simply the psychological reality of human beings thinking thoughts or having attitudes about something, and that things like France exist just in so far as this complex of psychological states does. The collecting property that is needed might be a very long and complex disjunctive property – for example, the property of either believing one thing or believing another or having a certain attitude, or . . . , and so on. But, regardless of the complexity, which may cause us epistemic headaches, this is all that the existence of entities like France comes to, metaphysically speaking. An example of this way of thinking might be Papineau's assertion that 'a norm against exogamy is nothing more than a shared attitude against marriage outside the group',[15] which locates the reality of a particular norm in shared attitudes. Although any purported reduction of France to beliefs and attitudes is unlikely to be as simple, the motivating thought might be much the same.

Perhaps I can start to evaluate this sort of suggestion by asking what beliefs and attitudes might yield the psychological properties true of those persons in the group with which France might be claimed to be reductively identical. As far as I know, no individualist has ever asked himself this question. Often, the thought just seems to be vague – that social entities are just individuals having certain attitudes or thinking certain thoughts, without there being any attempt to specify the content of these attitudes or beliefs.

Although I do not have an a priori proof for this claim, it seems most unlikely that the group with which it would be plausible to identify France could be any other than the group of individuals with some beliefs or attitudes *about France itself*. These might include beliefs that one is a national of France, or attitudes like loyalty to France. The beliefs and attitudes must not be so specific that any (many?) French persons fail to have them, but on the other hand they must not be so widespread that they might equally well be had by Germans or Italians. What beliefs could better insure that their holders include all and only the right persons than beliefs about France? Even here I say 'what could better ensure', because there are bound to be some Germans with false beliefs about their being French nationals, and even concerning whom a large number of other persons falsely believe they are French. Similarly, there may be a rather large number of French nationals who fail to have the requisite attitudes of loyalty to France, and a significant number of foreign spies who might have it. I know of no entity individualist discussion of these sorts of problems. Whether such difficulties are remediable or not, unless the beliefs and attitudes are about France, a successful identification of France with a group of persons with certain psychological properties seems unlikely to succeed.

Philip Pettit defends a methodological (but not a metaphysical) individualist position. In that defence, he remarks that one may have to explain certain social events or occurrences by referring to attitudes or beliefs, like the beliefs and attitudes of peasants that monetary payments promised certain prospects.[16] He notes that a holist might try to argue that, in characterising the beliefs and attitudes as ones with that content, monetary payments, 'we must

31

make further reference to institutions' (pp. 61-2). Pettit correctly points out that these belief and attitude contexts are non-extensional and hence no commitment to institutions or other social entities is implied by the truth of what one says. The truth of a claim that people have various beliefs about witches does not imply that there are any witches for them to have beliefs about; similarly, the claim that peasants had various beliefs about monetary payments does not entail that there are such things as monetary payments. The truth of the claim presupposes that the peasants possess the concept of a monetary payment, and hence it presupposes or implies that there is such a concept as the concept of a monetary payment. But it does not presuppose or imply that the concept has any instances.

I wish to offer two arguments against the possibility of the reductive (or even the non-reductive illuminating) identification of France with any group of persons who hold beliefs about France, or who have attitudes about France. The first argument supposes that beliefs about France are singular beliefs. The second argument does not rest on this presupposition, and hence is intended to demonstrate the conclusion I indicated whether the beliefs and attitudes about France are singular or general.

This first argument calls into question a very attractive picture about the way in which the empirical beliefs we have about the world and the empirical reality about which we have those beliefs are related. The picture is this: all of our empirical beliefs could be just as they are, even if nothing corresponded to them. Empirical reality and empirical beliefs are only contingently related; even if empirical reality were entirely different from the way that it is, I could continue to hold the very same empirical beliefs that I now hold.

For many empirical beliefs, the picture seems wrong. Arthur Pap considered the statement: 'There exist red surfaces (i.e. at least one).'[17] Since, according to Pap, 'red' cannot be defined verbally but only by ostension, 'in a universe containing no red objects or surfaces, "red" would be meaningless, and the existential statement, "there are red surfaces", would be not just false, but strictly insignificant'

(p. 237). Pap claims that, for ostensively defined terms, an existential belief that there is something of which the term is true could not be an intelligible belief at all unless empirical reality were such as to make it true.

The same point is made by many philosophers about proper names, names of natural kinds, or other expressions which function as rigid designators. Peter Unger, in his attack on the paradigm case argument, treats these cases as possible exceptions to his claim that 'the understanding you have of a word is essentially just a function of the state of the basis of your mind. . .'.[18] He concedes the possibility that, for these terms, 'whose character seems to resemble that of proper names', understanding these terms pre-supposes that empirical reality includes the things these terms purport to name. Of course, no real anti-sceptical conclusions can be drawn from Unger's concession, for the sceptic can always insist that, for all we can be certain of, we might not really understand those terms that we thought we did understand.

The first argument I wish to give is an adaptation of this same line of argument. It also presupposes, but does not prove, that we do have certain intelligible beliefs, and this is something that the convinced sceptic about the existence of irreducible social entities can deny without contradiction. The argument begins by distinguishing between two kinds of beliefs.

Beliefs are either singular, or general, or mixes of the two kinds. Pettit's example of the peasants' belief that monetary payments promised certain rewards is a general belief. If – to use a well-known example – I believe that there are lions, but have no particular lion in mind (indeed, I may never have been shown a lion, and may believe that there are lions on the strength of the reports of others), then my belief is a general belief, about no one thing in particular. If I believe of some particular lion, say Leo or the animal in the corner, that he is a lion, then my belief is singular. In holding a singular belief, I hold a belief about a particular object to which my belief relates me. Proper names like 'Leo' typically serve to indicate that the believer is so related to a particular object, but as Crispin Wright, echoing a point made by Keith

Donnellan, seeks to remind us, definite descriptions *can* serve to indicate precisely the same thing.[19]

A good test for singularity of a belief of A's, then, is this. All and only the singular beliefs of A can be represented as having this form: concerning x, A believes that p, where 'x' is replaced by a proper name or a definite description. Thus, if A believes that there are lions, then, concerning lions, A believes that there are some. But in this example, 'lions' is neither a proper name nor a definite description. On the other hand, if A believes that Leo is a lion, then concerning Leo, A believes that he is a lion. In this second case, 'Leo' is a name. This second case, unlike the first, is a case of singular belief.

The test for singularity of belief distinguishes between singular and non-singular uses of definite descriptions. Adopting an example from Wright, let us compare the beliefs of the policeman, 'ignorant of the identity of the killer, who surveys Smith's hideously mutilated corpse' and of Jones's confidant, 'who has it from Jones that he murdered Smith and knows independently of Jones' history of paranoid schizophrenia' (p. 99). Both the policeman and Jones's confidant have this belief: Smith's murderer is insane.

Presumably, Jones's confidant but not the policeman holds a singular belief. Our test makes this clear. Concerning Jones, Jones's confidant believes that he is the murderer of Smith and is insane. On the other hand, what the policeman believes is this: someone murdered Smith and that person is insane. The policeman's belief is a general belief, not a singular belief.

General beliefs, like the one which Pettit chose for illustrative purposes, do not, as he says, carry any existential commitment about the contents of the belief. But, on the other hand, if someone has a singular belief, for example that x is P, then it does follow that x exists. I separate the questions of the singularity of the belief and its transparency, and wish to commit myself only on the former issue. It might be that Jones has a singular belief that x is P, and $x = y$, yet false that he has the singular belief that y is P. But even if singular beliefs are opaque, in having such a belief, the believer is related to that entity or object about which he has the belief.

I recognise that there are problem cases for this view of belief, well known and deserving of more than the passing mention they will here receive. I am thinking of cases such as beliefs about Zeus, Pegasus, Santa Claus, and the alleged planet, Vulcan. These cases present us with a trilemma, no horn of which is easily graspable: either these are, despite appearances, not examples of intelligible beliefs at all, or they are, again despite appearances, examples of general beliefs, or they are bona fide examples of singular beliefs, and hence entail or presuppose the existence of some curious sort of subsistent entities. I am uncommitted about which is the least unacceptable way in which to deal with these cases, but opting for any of the horns of the trilemma would be consistent with my views on the distinction between singular and general belief.

Let us now return to the example of France. According to my contention, the beliefs and attitudes had by any group with whom it would be initially plausible to reductively identify France include beliefs and attitudes about France. It is true that the beliefs and attitudes might be about French things rather than about France (e.g. about French law being applicable in their case). But this, as I have already argued, comes to the same thing, since beliefs about French things are beliefs about things that come from or are made in or belong to, etc., France (e.g. French law is the law of France).

Are beliefs about France singular or general beliefs? They have every appearance of being singular beliefs, about some particular entity, France. But if these do prove to be singular beliefs, then the attempt to reductively identify France with a group of persons with some characteristic beliefs or attitudes about France will fail, on grounds of circularity. A necessary condition for there to be persons with singular beliefs about France is that France exists. Note that the argument for this does not just rely, in the trivial way that I earlier ruled out, on the alleged truth of the identity claim itself. Even if it were true that France could be identified with a group of persons with characteristic beliefs or attitudes or other mental states about France (and nothing in the present argument shows that this could not be so), the identity could not be reductive of ontic commitment for the reason I have given. Nor, for that matter could the identity be even non-reductive but illuminating, since the circularity is so immediate and obvious.

Appearances can be deceiving. Perhaps beliefs about France are general, not singular. If the beliefs in question are general after all, then no further existential commitments are entailed merely by supposing that there are such beliefs. If France can be identified with a group of persons who hold certain general beliefs, then no charge of circularity would arise, and the identification could prove genuinely reductive.

What would someone have to show, in order to demonstrate that, despite appearances, these beliefs about France were general beliefs? The person would have to show that the belief that France is P was, for example, just the general belief that there is one and only one thing which is D, and it is P. Now, a necessary condition for showing this to be so is that there be a definite description, 'the one and only D', such that 'France is the one and only D' is analytic. It is important to note that 'France is the one and only D' would have to be analytic, not just either necessary or knowable a priori. If this were analytic, then the belief that France is P could be shown to be equivalent to the belief that the one and only thing which is D is P, and that could be construed as the general belief that there is one and only one thing which is D and it is P. Such a general belief is of course existential in the sense that it is a belief about existence, but the point about this belief is that it does not entail the existence of something which is uniquely D, and this difference would be enough to permit the identification of France with the group of persons with these beliefs to escape the charge of circularity.

So the question that we must now answer is this: Is there any definite description such that 'France is the one and only D' is an analytic truth? I assert that there is none. Suppose, for instance, that someone were to claim that 'France is the nation of which Napoleon was emperor' is analytic. We could dismiss this, and any similar claim, with the following sort of coherent story. There has been a systematic distortion of the historical documents and hence of the history books by militants of the Up-Gaul Movement. We have thereby come to believe that Napoleon, much admired by members of that society, was the emperor of France, when in fact he was emperor of Spain. I claim that if this logically possible story were true, then 'Napoleon was emperor of France' would be false, because it would say, of France, that Napoleon was emperor of it, and this, in the supposed circumstances, would not be so.

If 'Napoleon was emperor of France' were analytic, then in order for it to still be true in the supposed circumstances, it would have to say, of Spain, that Napoleon was emperor of it. 'France' would then designate Spain, and presumably we should have to find some alternative way of designating France. But this is absurd, because names like 'France' and 'Spain' do not behave in this way. The way in which we designate some particular social substance is (often) by their names, and we can, in those cases, learn sometimes obvious but always synthetic truths about the named social substance (with the exception of truths like 'France is France', derivable by substitution from logical truths).

Some may wonder how beliefs about France, or indeed about any social entity, can be singular. One prominent idea about singularity of belief connects singularity with a causal theory of reference; for example, a paradigm case of a singular belief might be a belief about a particular person, reference to whom is secured not through descriptions but in a direct encounter, an ostension, or an immediate acquaintance which fixes the meaning of the name. One may wonder what sense can be given to the idea of a direct encounter with France (recall that we are thinking of the social substance and not the geographical expanse or area).

I do not wish to discuss fully various theories of reference and how they might bear on the possibility of singular beliefs about social substances. However, singular beliefs about social substances seem certainly no more difficult to understand than singular beliefs about abstract objects. The thought that numbers are abstract objects and yet that we can have singular beliefs about them is not uncommon, although admittedly it is also not uncontroversial. Since abstract objects cannot be relata in causal relations, if we can have singular beliefs about them, there must be a way of securing reference to them, other than the way in which reference can be secured in the case of persons or middle-sized physical objects.[20] So it may not even be necessary to insist on causality as the route by which all bona fide reference is secured.

If beliefs about France are singular, then in so far as I hold such a belief, I stand in a certain relation, the belief relation, to an object, France. My argument in this section is conditional on accepting that there can be intelligible beliefs about France, as well as accepting that all beliefs are either singular or general or mixes of the two, and that a belief about France is not a general belief. The individualist I am discussing wanted reductively to identify France with a group of persons who hold beliefs and attitudes about France, so he will certainly accept that there are such intelligible beliefs.

I have, I hope, shown that Pettit's too easy dismissal of existential commitments in the case of a general belief like the one about monetary payments cannot be repeated for cases of singular belief. In these cases, there are existential commitments within the belief and attitude contexts. Since this is so, the identification of France with any group of persons who hold certain beliefs or attitudes about France cannot be reductive, since the beliefs and attitudes themselves presuppose the existence of the entity to be reduced. Any such identification, even if true, would be circular.

My second argument against the reduction of France to a group of persons with some set of beliefs or attitudes does not assume that these beliefs and attitudes about France are singular. Suppose beliefs about France are general. Suppose, contrary to what I have argued, that when someone believes that France is P, he believes something with this logical form: 'There is one and only one thing which is D, and it is P', because 'France' means 'the one and only thing which is D'. Could France be reductively identified with a group of persons who hold these general sorts of beliefs? As a working example, let's suppose that 'France' means 'the one and only nation of which Napoleon was the emperor'. Could France just be reductively identified with the group of persons who believe that there is only one thing which is a nation of which Napoleon was the emperor, and that they are nationals of it?

Let's say that a general belief of the form, 'There is one and only one thing which is D, and it is P', is descriptively false, or d-false, iff its falsity arises from the fact that the one and only thing which is D is not P. On the other hand, the belief is referentially false, or r-false, iff its falsity arises as a consequence of there not being one and only one thing which is D. R-falsity itself has two subcases. There may be more than one thing which is D, or there may be nothing whatever which is D. I am interested only in the latter case, and shall have only it in mind when I speak of r-falsity.

Consider the general beliefs that are to be ascribed to that group of persons with which France is to be reductively identified. Are there any characteristics of these beliefs that we can discern, regardless of which specific beliefs are included? One thing, I think, is clear. These beliefs, whichever they are, cannot be r-false. It is not easy to credit the idea that they could be d-false either, but there is not the same impossibility about this as there is about their r-falsity. Since we are seeking a reductive identification for France, rather than attempting to eliminate France from our ontology altogether, we are assuming that France exists. Put it this way: a necessary condition for reductively identifying France with any entity whatever is that France exists. But if France exists, then beliefs about France, even if they are general beliefs, are r-true beliefs.

Could France, then, be reductively identified with a group of persons who hold certain general r-true beliefs about France? France could, I maintain, be identical with such a group, but not reductively so. Again suppose that the general belief in question, ascribed to the members of the group, is that there is one and only one thing which is a nation of which Napoleon was the emperor, and that they are nationals of it. That people believe that there is one and only one thing which is a nation of which Napoleon was the emperor and that they are nationals of it does *not* presuppose that any nation exists. But that they have this belief *and* that the belief is r-true does presuppose or entail that this nation exists. It follows from the fact that they have this r-true belief that there is such a nation; there cannot be such an r-true belief unless France, the one and only thing which is a nation of which Napoleon was the emperor, exists. The identification of France with a group of persons who hold certain r-true beliefs about France would be circular, and hence not reductive, since the existence of the reducing entity (the group of persons with certain r-true beliefs about France) presupposes the existence of the very same entity that we are trying to reduce (France).

My argument, then, is that the following identification claim would be circular: 'France = the group of persons with such-and-such r-true beliefs, etc., about France.' I argued before that in a purported reductive identification of Fs with Gs, the circularity charge cannot be sustained merely on the grounds that, if the identification claim is true, then the existence of a G is necessary and sufficient for the existence of an F and hence the existence of a G must presuppose the existence of an F. If circularity charges could be sustained on these grounds alone, then no identification, if true, could fail to be circular. My argument however rests on the specific choice of reducing entity, rather than just on the fact that some entity, no matter which, is claimed to be identical with the entity to be reduced.

It is obviously essential to my argument that the fact that the beliefs of the persons are r-true figures in the description of those beliefs. Is this requirement in fact justifiable? After all, many of the features of the beliefs need not figure in the description. For example, suppose the beliefs are expressed in French, or are identical with certain brain states. But even if these were truths about the beliefs, it certainly is not required that we include the information in the identification claim we are considering.

But the r-truth of the beliefs is not like those other supposed facts about the beliefs. For the purposes of the identification, this is not a contingent fact about the beliefs. France might be identical with a group of persons who have certain beliefs about France, whether or not the beliefs were expressed in French or were identical with brain states. But the beliefs of the persons, if they are beliefs about France, *must* be r-true if France is identical with a group of persons with those beliefs. Therefore, in the identification of France, the r-truth of the beliefs about France must be included in the description of the beliefs.

This second argument that I have now offered has a wider application than its use in the case of France might suggest. The purpose of reductive identification is not just to avoid irreducible ontic commitment to some particular social substance like France. It is, presumably, to avoid irreducible ontic commitment to any social entity whatever, where this might include not only social substances, but also social events, processes, and so on. Since we are dealing in this chapter only with the question of social entities and not social properties, we can permit our individualist the retention of irreducible social properties. But what he does wish to accomplish is to jettison commitment to irreducible social entities, which we might construe as anything other than individuals or physical things (and perhaps mathematical objects) over which we should have to quantify in a formalisation of social science or our ordinary discourse about society. Consider for example this claim by Hugh Mellor: one can reduce 'social facts to people's beliefs about social facts . . . the social behaviour of groups can be so derived, from how people think and feel about social facts.'[21]

Not all social facts are about a social entity, for some social facts are about individual entities, and merely assert of them that they have some social property (e.g. the social fact that some individual is an alderman). But consider only the subset of social facts that are facts about some social entity (whether substances, events, processes, etc.). If my argument worked against the attempt to reductively identify France with the group of persons who hold certain general beliefs about France, it will work against any attempt to reduce any social entity, or facts about it, to how people think and feel about that entity or about any facts about that entity. In these cases, the argument is the same as the one I gave above. The beliefs or attitudes – 'how people think and feel' – must be r-true (we can easily extend the notion of r-truth to apply to attitudes) if they are to serve as the reductive identifiers for social entities, and if they are r-true, the charge of circularity can be sustained.

It may be helpful to compare these circular identifications with some that are non-circular, in spite of using beliefs about something with which to reductively identify something. Consider, for example, David Armstrong's reductive identification of appearances or perceptions with beliefs or dispositions to believe things about physical objects.[22] The form of such a reductive identification is this: As are (sets of) beliefs about Bs. No charge of circularity is necessarily sustainable in this kind of case. But the case we have been examining, and that Mellor proposes, is the reductive identification of As with beliefs about As. This form of reductive identification is bound to seem trivial, and this intuition of its triviality arises from the fact that it is circular. The triviality does not arise just from the fact that we must reuse the concept of an A in the right-hand side of the identification, for this is not the sort of circularity we have been discussing. The point is, quite generally, that if we are reductively identifying As with anything at all, rather than eliminating them, as we do in the case of demons, unicorn horns, and caloric fluids, then there must be As. Therefore, if the identification takes the form of As with (sets of persons with?) r-true beliefs about As, then this is circular, and hence not genuinely reductive, not just because the right-hand side of the identification reuses the concept of an A, but because the right-hand side presupposes that there is some thing of which the concept of an A is true, and hence that there are As.

A possibility that my argument does not defeat is the reductive identification of a social entity, or a social fact about that entity, with how people think and feel about some *other* social entity or facts about them. This would have the form: As are nothing else but beliefs about Bs, where the concept of an A and the concept of a B are both social. This would not be circular, for there is no argument available to me to show that the beliefs about Bs must be r-true beliefs. Although I have no a priori argument against this, I cannot think how any such reductive identification could be right. We should have to locate the 'reality' of a social entity in beliefs about some other entity, whether social or not, and this seems hard to understand. There is also the sheer difficulty of meeting the requirement of extensional equivalence: how could France be reductively identified with persons holding beliefs and attitudes about anything other than France itself? Intuitively, the group of believers which has any chance of being the group with which France can be reductively identified is the group of those persons who are, in fact, French, and it is therefore unlikely that the believers about anything other than something about France are going to be just the believers one needs for the reductive identification. I do not have an a priori argument to show that this must be so, but I think one can say that the idea that the group of believers one needs could have other beliefs and attitudes, which are not about the very entity for which the reductive identification is being sought, has a very low initial plausibility. Or, recall Papineau's suggestion that exogamy is nothing more than a shared attitude about marriage outside the group. Exogamy just is, by definition, marriage outside the group, so the attitudes or beliefs in question are themselves about exogamy. Could, as Papineau claimed, the institution of exogamy be identified with (sets of persons who share?) general beliefs and attitudes about exogamy? On the one hand, surely any identification with any initial plausibility must include beliefs about exogamy, the very entity for which the reduction is being sought, for how could exogamy just be beliefs and attitudes about anything else? On the other hand, how could such an identification, even if true, be reductive? If one is seeking a reductive identification for exogamy, exogamy exists. If it exists, beliefs about exogamy are r-true beliefs, and that they are r-true is a necessary condition for there being any reductive identification for exogamy at all. But if the beliefs are r-true, then they presuppose the existence of exogamy, so that any such identification, even if true, is circular and hence non-reductive.

I conclude that the third candidate for the role of collecting property for the group of persons with that property (with which France was to be reductively identified) fares no better than its predecessors. This third candidate, the psychological property of having certain beliefs and attitudes, is perhaps the favourite candidate of individualists.

I believe that, taken as a whole, this chapter has rendered the acceptance of premiss (4) rational, since I have discussed and dismissed the most obvious candidates for the role of reducing entity. I have already said that I cannot conclusively demonstrate that my argument is sound, for numerous reasons, but I believe that I have given some strong reasons for thinking that it is. In part, this is a matter of not being able to show that no such reducing candidate is adequate, for example that there are no acceptable non-extensional but also non-social entities, or that there are no other acceptable groups of persons. I think that what is perhaps surprising is just how implausible the obvious candidates turn out to be, on the slightest careful inspection. I therefore believe that I have given some good reasons for thinking that irreducible social substances, like France, must be included in any ontological catalogue of what there is. If so, it is reasonable to believe that entity individualism, as a metaphysical rather than a methodological thesis in the philosophy of social science, is simply false.

Finally, some philosophers accept this slogan: no entity without criteria of identity. One might wonder what criteria of identity would be appropriate for social entities of various kinds. Gregory Currie has suggested, in a recent paper, that social institutions a and b are identical iff a and b have all the same effects on individuals.[23] Although I would not wish to commit myself on the details of the specific proposal, I accept the desirability of giving some criteria of this sort.

CHAPTER 2

Social wholes and parts

No social entity is identical with any individual entity, or set of individual entities. As I said in the first chapter, it is obvious that there is some close relation between social entities and human individuals. If social entities exist, it cannot just be a contingent fact that some individuals do so as well. What is this close relation, if it is not that of identity? Many who have written in the philosophy of the social sciences have thought that one of the important relations that holds between at least some social entities and the human beings who are their members is the relation of a whole to its parts. So prominent is this thought that the side in the dispute concerning the ontological status of social entities which wishes to assign them some irreducible metaphysical reality is usually referred to as 'holism'. Quinton, for instance, writes: 'I do not take the relation of a social object to its human constituents to be that of a logical construction to its elements. It is, rather, that of a whole to its parts.'[1] Macdonald and Pettit claim, 'What we have been saying about groups is that they are wholes composed out of persons as parts.'[2] Arthur Danto *defines*, provisionally, social entities as those 'containing individual human beings amongst their parts'.[3] Nor is this idea restricted to those who write in the philosophy of social science. Paul Oppenheim and Hilary Putnam, in an influential article,[4] defend the idea 'as a working hypothesis' that 'unitary science can be attained through cumulative micro-reduction' (p. 8). A necessary condition for the micro-reduction of science B_2 by science B_1 is that 'the objects in the universe of discourse of B_2 are wholes which possess a decomposition into proper parts all of which belong to the universe of discourse of B_1' (p. 6). The authors envisage the micro-reduction of sociology to theories concerning individuals, the micro-reduction of the latter to cellular biology, and cellular biology to molecular chemistry, thence to atomic theory, and finally to elementary particle physics (p. 9 and ff.). What they assume (with only the briefest of discussions on p. 11) is that individuals are the parts of groups in the same sense in which atoms are the parts of molecules.

Organic metaphors, in which state or society was conceived of as an organism whose parts, like the limbs and organs of the body, were persons, were already common in classical and medieval political philosophy. The main purpose of this chapter is to examine this influential idea, and to argue that it is fundamentally misconceived. Whatever relations human beings bear to social entities, the relation of being a part of is not one of them. I defend the commonsensical thought that individuals are the members of social groups, and I claim that this membership relation has sometimes been misidentified as the relation of a part to a whole. A subsidiary purpose of this chapter is to examine and resolve some difficulties in mereology, the logic of wholes and parts, to see whether or not these have any consequence for the philosophy of social science.

In this chapter, I build on the results of the first chapter. I therefore take particular groups, nations, clubs, associations, and so on, to be entities. It is worth mentioning, however, that this chapter would have interest in its own right, even if the reader should reject my claims in the first chapter. This chapter is directed against those who think that social entities are wholes with humans as their parts, and those who think this must be assuming that these things – groups, nations, clubs – are entities, since nothing can be a whole without being an entity of some sort. Entity holism is not only an assumption of this chapter, but also of those against whom this chapter is aimed.

I am not much interested in the ordinary language use of such expressions as 'whole' and 'part'. Although I argue that individuals do not bear to social entities the relation of being a part of, I would not of course deny that we sometimes say with propriety such things as that a person is part of some group. However, I construe such ways of speaking as claiming that the individual is a member of the group in question, or that he belongs to it, and not as claiming that the individual stands in the mereological relation to the social group of being one of its parts. I think, that is, that the social relation of being a member of, or of belonging to, and the mereological relation of being a part of, are distinct, and that this can be shown by giving the different principles involved in the application of the two relations. It does not matter from my point of view that we may sometimes refer to the social relation of being a member of by the use of part-whole language.

When speaking of mereological parts and wholes, I use the expression 'is a part of' of entities which may be or become parts of wholes, as well as of entities which are actually the parts of some whole. I think that ordinary usage sanctions this, for I can certainly talk of the dismembered parts of a person strewn across a battlefield. For those who might think that ordinary usage does not sanction this, let 'part' for them, as I use it, be a technical term of art. I rely on readers' pre-theoretic intuitions about wholes. Some assemblages of parts can make wholes (e.g. the parts of a clock), and some assemblages do not, even when brought into spatial contiguity (my belt, Victoria Station, and your lunch).

Finally, before I begin the argument proper of this chapter, I would like to make an important general remark about its methodology. On numerous occasions, I assert that some general mereological principle is true. All such principles about which I make this claim will be, I hope, intuitively plausible. Wherever possible, I adduce examples. My strategy is to show that human individuals cannot be the parts of the social groups to which they belong or of which they are the members, on the grounds that if they were, there is some otherwise acceptable mereological principle that would not be true of them. It is, of course, always possible to take the high road in arguments of this type, and assert that since individuals just are the parts of social groups, the otherwise acceptable mereological principle(s) I claimed were true are in fact false, because there are bona fide cases of wholes and parts which are exceptions to them. I think that this sort of move, although perfectly possible, is unwise, because under-motivated. What I claim as mereological principles hold for all undisputed cases of wholes and parts. If they do not hold for some controversial case, the wisest course is to retain the principle and infer that the controversial case is not in fact a bona fide example of a whole and its parts.

There is a spin-off from regarding the strategy of this chapter in this light. Are the mereological principles that I cite in this chapter necessarily true or contingently true? If they are necessarily true, then it is of course logically impossible that anything of which they are not true be a whole with parts. But suppose some of these principles are true, but only contingently so. In that case, it would be wrong to say that it was impossible for anything of which they fail to be true to be a whole with parts. However, even if only contingently true of all uncontroversial cases of wholes and parts, we are still provided with a good reason for denying that a controversial or non-paradigmatic case is a bona fide case of a whole and its parts, if those mereological principles are not true of it. It is in this spirit that I would wish this chapter to be understood. Of course, any reader who thinks that my mereological principles, if true, must be necessarily true, is welcome to construe my chapter as demonstrating the stronger point.

What social entities are wholes whose parts are individuals?

I begin my argument proper with this question: What are the social entities such that it is even initially plausible to hold that human individuals are their parts? Sometimes it is thought that individuals are the parts of all social entities if

the parts of any, as Quinton implies in the quotation with which I began the chapter. But of course this might be a truth about some social entities without being a truth about all, as Macdonald and Pettit suppose when they restrict their claim to social *groups*. I think that there are at least some clear cases of social entities whose parts are not persons, and that it will be useful to start by considering these cases.

The case I have in mind is France. I have already mentioned in the first chapter that sometimes we seem to use 'France' to denote a geographical area and sometimes to denote a social substance. We do the former when we say 'I visited France last summer', the latter when we say 'France is a charter member of the United Nations'. I remind the reader of this, since the question of whether persons are the parts of France might be taken as a question about the relation between individuals and a geographical entity or between individuals and a social entity.

It might be thought that this was a true mereological principle:

(1) If x is a whole and if $a_1 \ldots a_n$ are all of its parts, and if x, $a_1 \ldots a_n$ are spatially locatable, then the spatial location of the whole, x, is identical with the sum of the spatial locations of $a_1 \ldots a_n$.

Where else could a whole be, if not where its parts are? (1) does not entail that all, wholes and parts are spatially locatable, nor even rule out the possibility that either the whole or the parts could have spatial location but not the other. (1) only asserts that if the whole and the parts all have spatial location, then the spatial location of the former is identical with the sum of the spatial locations of the latter. This seems plausible enough. A person's body is where his arms, legs, head, etc are; a clock is where its casing, springs, winding mechanism, etc. are.

I assume that it is uncontroversial that both France and individual French persons have spatial location. Even if France qua social substance cannot be identified with any geographical location, it certainly *has* a location. Moreover, even if persons can exist disembodied and hence without spatial location, such disembodied persons are not the nationals of any state. If (1) were true, it would follow that the French cannot be the parts or at any rate the only parts of France. Consider two phenomena, that of spatial discontinuity and spatial emptiness. First, the French are spatially discontinuous from one another, in all but the most intimate of moments. I accept that there can be genuine wholes with spatially discontinuous parts. Indeed, France might have spatially discontinuous parts – e.g. if the sea between mainland France and Corsica were not itself a part of France. But even if France is spatially discontinuous, it does not arise merely as a consequence of the fact that the French are spatially discontinuous from one another. Second, as for the phenomenon of emptiness, large areas of France may be uninhabited, so that France can exist even where no French person does. But (1) says that a whole cannot exist where no part of it exists. Since France does exist where no French person does, it should follow that the French are not the parts of France, or anyway that they cannot be the only parts of France.

Unfortunately, it is not at all clear that (1) is true. Suppose (as presumably one version of atomic theory held) that physical objects, whose parts are atoms, were composed from those atoms in such a way that large expanses, relatively speaking, of empty space separated the atoms from one another. The atoms are spatially discontinuous from one another, but the physical object of which they are the parts may not have a discontinuous spatial existence. The physical object occupies the whole of some area, the parts (the atoms) occupy spatial locations scattered within that area but less than the whole area occupied by the physical object. Thus it seems that wholes can be where none of its parts are. Perhaps France is to the French in the same way in which a physical object would be to such atomic parts.

I am not at all sure that this example of a physical object and its atomic parts does succeed in showing that (1) is false. First, it may be that the parts of the physical object are both the atoms and the intervening spaces, in the way in which the hole is a part, indeed a most important part, of a

Polo mint, Lifesaver, and bagel.[5] This move might help us to defend (1), but would not help us in our use of it in the case of France, since it would allow us to explain away the phenomena of discontinuity and emptiness by counting the unoccupied spaces as well as the French as the parts of France. Second, even if we do refuse to count empty space as a part of something, we might decide to deny that the whole, the physical object, does after all occupy more space than its atomic parts do. It might have been believed that a physical object occupied some entire spatial expanse, before we came to understand about the spatial whereabouts of its atomic constituents. But after we learn about their spatial positions and reflect on the matter, it may seem quite plausible to deny the commonsense belief that the physical object occupies the whole spatial expanse that it appears to occupy. This might be brought out by imagining another physical object 'inserted' into the first, such that the atomic parts of the second object just fit into the spaces between the atomic parts of the first, with the exception that they share the atomic parts which make up the (shared) surface of the two objects. This possibility might get us to see that, appearances notwithstanding, each object cannot occupy the entire spatial expanse, but only the spatial locations occupied by its atomic parts, with the two objects I described sharing some spatial positions because they share some parts. This defence of (1), unlike the first, should help us in the case of France. Even if we accept the view that objects are spatially discontinuous if their parts are, no one will accept that France is spatially discontinuous merely on the grounds that its nationals are, and hence it would follow that the French are not the parts or only parts of France.

We can avoid deciding whether (1) is true or false by weakening (1) to obtain an uncontroversially true principle which is still strong enough for my purposes:

(1*) If x is a whole and if $a_1 \ldots a_n$ are all of its parts, and if x, $a_1 \ldots a_n$ are spatially locatable, then the spatial location of the whole, x, at least includes the spatial locations of $a_1 \ldots a_n$.

(1*) says that no whole can fail to be where its parts are. It

51

may be that a whole can be where none of its parts are, but it must be at least where its parts are. By using (1*), we can show that the French are not even among the parts of France. French people can live abroad, say in Iceland, and can do so in some official French capacity (as ambassadors, for example). But it does not follow that some part of France can be spatially located in Iceland. This consideration shows not just that the French cannot be all the parts of France there are – which is perhaps the best that the considerations of spatial discontinuity and emptiness could have shown – but, more strongly, that the French cannot even be among the parts of France.

On reflection, it seems obvious that the parts of France are either the administrative departments, if we take 'France' to refer to a social entity, or geographical regions, if we take 'France' to refer to an area or territory. And if these are its parts, (1*) is certainly true of them, because if I give the spatial location of either the departments or the various geographical regions, I thereby do give at least part of the spatial location of France. So if any social entities have humans as parts, France is not amongst them.

I doubt whether anyone would really be inclined to believe that the French were the parts, or among the parts, of France. On the other hand, it is rather more common to hear the idea that individuals are the parts of clubs, organisations, associations, etc. to which they belong. I think that it is an error to think of individuals as the parts of these things as well, but in order to see this, (1*) has to be supplemented with an additional mereological principle:

(2) If x is a whole and if $a_1 \ldots a_n$ are all of its parts, then if $a_1 \ldots a_n$ have spatial location, x has spatial location.

(2) would, I think, remain true even if the conditional assertion that occurs in the consequence of (2) were strengthened to a bi-conditional, but I prefer to defend the weakest principle necessary for my argument, and hence will defend (2) only in the form in which I have stated it. Later in the chapter, I will introduce further mereological principles about the spatial characteristics of parts and

wholes, (9), (11), and (12). These too can be strengthened in the way in which I said that (2) could and still remain true, but I similarly assert and defend them in the weaker form.

Introducing (2), (9), (11), and (12) in the manner in which I do might make them appear to the reader as arbitrary. I do not believe that any of them is in any way *ad hoc*. Each of them gets at an essential ingredient in the idea that something is a part of something else. In general, there are many properties that can be possessed by every one of the parts of a whole and yet not by the whole made up of those parts. An example is the property of being the proper part of a whole, true of all the proper parts of a whole but untrue of the whole unless it, in its turn, is the proper part of some larger whole. But the spatial characteristics mentioned in (2), (9), (11), and (12) are not like this. For example, the property of having a spatial location, the property mentioned in (2), is such that if all the parts have this property, then the whole formed with these parts must have it. This fact, that the spatiality of the parts carries over to the spatiality of the whole, is one way in which the mereological relation of being a part of can be distinguished from some other relations, like the relationship of set membership.

Ask yourself if the International Red Cross or the Association of University Teachers has spatial location or not (of course, their headquarters do, but do they?). I have found that intuitions about this differ, so I will construct my argument in the form of a dilemma: either these things do or do not have spatial location. Let's grasp the second horn of the dilemma first. If clubs, organisations, and associations have no spatial location, we can argue as follows. Human beings do, uncontroversially, have spatial location (at least they do uncontroversially at some times, and in particular at the times when they are members of these clubs, associations, and organisations). According to (2), whatever human beings are the parts of must have spatial location. Thus, the rejection of spatial location for clubs, associations, and organisations entails that human beings cannot be, or be among, their mereological parts.

On the first horn of the dilemma, we concede that these social entities do have a genuine spatial location. Using an argument similar to the one I used in the case of France, one can show that their spatial location may not include the spatial location of their members. Imagine a tour of a country with no national Red Cross (Albania perhaps) by a group of individuals who stand in any relationship to the Red Cross one might like to single out – Red Cross workers, or officials, or executives, or whatever. Let their tour of the country be in an official Red Cross capacity. Locating those individuals in that country for however long a period does not necessarily bring it about that the Red Cross can also be located in Albania. That is, the spatial location of the Red Cross, assuming it has one, may not even include the spatial locations of designated individuals who bear some special relationship to it. They can be where it is not. By (1*), it follows that individuals cannot be the parts of such entities as the Red Cross, Equity, the Association of University Teachers, and so on. Again on reflection, it seems plain that if these social entities do have spatial location, they are to be located wherever they have branches or affiliates, and that these latter exist wherever they have been duly constituted as existing. It is possible for an organisation to have an inactive branch or affiliate at some place, and hence to be at that place, where it has no members at all. So I conclude that individuals are not the parts of clubs, associations, or organisations, whether or not these later have spatial location.

Are individuals the parts of groups?

Perhaps there is some other social entity of which individuals are the parts, even if not the parts of the ones I have discussed hitherto. Sometimes the suggestion has been that individuals are the parts of society, and this idea seems sufficiently different to warrant separate consideration.

What does talk of society come to in this context? To speak of French society rather than France is either a way of speaking about a specific social structure, as defined by a set of relations (or perhaps a type of a set of relations), or a way of talking about the sundry groups of individuals who are related by those relations. If we assert that French society was more highly stratified in the nineteenth century than it is today, we are saying something about the social relations in which those groups of persons stood. If we say that French society placed a high value on honour, we are saying something about a group of persons and their beliefs. For our purposes, the first alternative is trivially uninteresting, because neither sets of relations nor types thereof have mereological parts. More promising is the second alternative, the idea that individuals are the parts of the groups to which they belong, and this recalls the suggestion made by Macdonald and Pettit that groups are wholes whose parts are persons. It is worth noting that this is a suggestion distinct from the ones we discussed earlier, because (1*) and (2) will not yield a conclusive argument against this idea. Social groups, like persons, seem to have spatial location; or, at any rate, even if our ordinary mode of thinking about them does not clearly compel such ascriptions, it also does not clearly refuse such spatial ascriptions either. Moreover, if social groups do have spatial location, it seems quite natural to identify it with the sum of the spatial locations of the group's members. There is nothing counterintuitive about admitting that some group like the Romany might have part of its spatial location in Iceland if there are some Gypsies there, in the way in which it was counterintuitive to locate part of France in Iceland on the same grounds. Indeed, if there are French persons in Iceland, then it seems acceptable to believe that part of the group of French persons is located in Iceland, in spite of the fact that no part of France can be so located. So if there is anything wrong in the idea that individuals are the parts of the groups to which they belong, nothing we have said so far permits us to say what that error is.

Examples of social groups, in the sense I intend, are teams, tribes, social classes, and families. Such examples would include: the Celtic football team, the Jewish people, the Apache tribe, the British middle class, and the Rothschild family. Social groups of persons are unlike sets of persons, in that at least some changes of membership are identity-preserving for social groups. I refer the reader back to my discussion in the first chapter, in which I distinguished more fully between groups and extensional entities like sets.

Some additional putative principles of mereology

Are the individuals the parts of the social groups to which they belong? Before I try to answer this question, I want to discuss in a general way some putative mereological principles. Some I think will prove to be genuine, others spurious. Here are some additional principles for consideration:

(3)   If a and b are wholes and if a = b, then a and b have the same parts.
(3*) If a and b are wholes and a and b have the same parts, then a = b.
(4)   Wholes are necessary for the existence of their parts.
(5)   Parts are necessary for the existence of the whole of which they are the parts.
(6)   The whole is greater than the sum of its parts.

(6) is true, at least under one plausible interpretation that I will mention later. I take (3) to be uncontroversially true, since it is an instance of the indiscernibility of identicals. Consider an analogous principle for groups:

(3G) If a and b are groups and a = b, then a and b have the same members.

(3G) is also uncontroversially true, since it too is an instance of the indiscernibility of identicals. One might wonder how (3) and (3G) can be true, since both groups and (as I shall soon argue) wholes can remain numerically identical in spite of at least some changes in membership or of parts. Let a be a whole (group) at some earlier time t and let b be the same whole (group) at some later time t'. Suppose in addition that there has been some part replacement (or change in membership) between t and t'. Can't a = b, in spite of the fact that they have different parts (members)?

56

On reflection, a and b have the *same* parts (members), if this is appropriately temporally qualified. A has certain parts at t, and b has different parts at t'. But if a = b, then a has at t' b's parts (it must, because it is b), and b has at t a's parts (it must, because it is a). The same is true if we substitute 'members' for 'parts' in the previous sentence. Neither the possibility of membership changes for groups nor part changes for wholes raises any difficulty for the indiscernibility of identicals, once the having of parts or members is temporally qualified.

(3*), the converse of (3), is false. So too is the converse of (3G):

(3G*)   If a and b are groups and a and b have the same members, then a = b.

(3*) and (3G*) assert that indiscernibility with respect to parts and members entails identity, and this is not true. Why can't they be saved, as were (3) and (3G), by the insertion of the appropriate temporal qualification? In the case of (3G*), the principle of the identity of member-indiscernibles, this is because two distinct groups can have the same members at all times. In the case of (3*), the principle of the identity of part-indiscernibles, the reason is different.

Imagine some pieces of Lego set, such that if they are assembled in one way they compose a table and if assembled in another way they make up a chair. In spite of the fact that the table and chair have the same parts, the table and chair are not identical, and this would seem to confirm that (3*) is false.

But one might hope to save (3*) by a temporal qualification, even if (3G*) cannot be similarly saved. At any specific time, the pieces of Lego must be arranged in one way rather than any other. Specifying a time in effect means permitting only one from the many possible arrangements of the parts. So if a and b are wholes with the same parts at the same time, then doesn't a = b? Isn't the principle of the identity of part-indiscernibles, when temporally qualified, true after all? Two distinct wholes can have the same parts at different times (because the parts can be differently arranged), but one might suppose that (3*) suitably qualified is true because there cannot be distinct wholes with the same parts at the same time.

Nicholas Rescher correctly argues that (3*) cannot be saved, but he says that this is because 'the extensionality property, which entails that wholes are the same if they possess the same parts, rules out those senses of "part-whole" in which the organisation of the parts, in addition to the mere parts themselves, is involved.'[6] However, it is not organisational arrangement by itself that creates problems for (3*), since we have just seen in the case of spatio-temporal wholes how this can be catered for by the insertion of a temporal qualification, which would seem to 'save' the 'extensionality property'.

Rescher's own example of a whole for which the 'extensionality property' is not true is a whole which is an abstract object: 'Different sentences can consist of the same words.' If all wholes existed in space and time, such that the parts of every whole could be arranged in only one way at a time, (3*) could be saved by the insertion of an appropriate temporal qualification. But, as I shall argue more fully later, some wholes are abstract obejcts, whose existence is neither spatial nor temporal. Two novels or two sentences (the types, not the tokens) can exist coevally with the same parts differently arranged. Two distinct sentence types can be made up of precisely the same words (word types) but in different order. There is no temporal qualification that will help in this sort of case, because of the a-temporal existence of the wholes concerned.

Rescher's example of a case that defeats (3*) is correct, but not for the reason he gives. It is not organisation or arrangement of the parts of just any whole that presents insuperable difficulties for (3*), but only the organisation or arrangement of parts of abstract wholes. Thus, unlike (3) and (3G), which are true when appropriately temporally qualified, neither the converse of (3) nor the converse of (3G) can be saved in the same way. The converse of (3G), (3G*), cannot be saved by a temporal qualification because two groups can have the same members at all times. The converse of (3), (3*), cannot be saved by a temporal qualification because of the existence of wholes which have neither spatial nor temporal existence.

(4) is the principle of hological essentialism; (5) is the principle of mereological essentialism. One way in which (4) and (5) might be thought to bear on the question of the relation between persons and groups is this. It seems at least logically possible that I might have existed, with however an altered personality, without being a member of at least some of the groups to which I in fact do belong. Moreover, as I have already claimed, social groups are unlike sets, since they are able to continue numerically the same in spite of some changes in membership. Given these two facts, if either hological or mereological essentialism were true, the relation between individuals and social groups could not be the relation of parts to a whole.

Are either (4) or (5) true? They can be stated less ambiguously as:

(4*) for any times t and t', for any actual or possible
      objects x and y, and for any actual or possible
      states of affairs c and c', if x is a part of y at t in c,
      then if x exists in c' at t', x is a part of y at t' in c'.

(5*) For any times t and t', for any actual or possible
      objects x and y, and for any actual or possible
      states of affairs c and c', if y has x as a part in c at
      t, then if y exists in c' at t', then y has x as a part at
      t' in c'.

My statement of the two forms of essentialism is modelled on Plantinga's formulation of mereological essentialism (which he in fact rejects),[7] but strengthened so that if any possible object is a part or has a part, then it is that part or has that part in every possible world in which it exists. On Plantinga's formulation, as well as on Chisholm's version against which Plantinga writes,[8] if some object is a part or has a part in the actual world, then it is that part or has that part in every possible world in which it exists. This weaker thesis is consistent, but not well-motivated. On the Chisholm-Plantinga version of mereological essentialism, this actual table, which has this leg, has just this leg in every possible world in which it exists. But, in some merely possible world, there is a table, and it is possible that that very table exists in some other possible world with a different leg. But why should actual and merely possible wholes differ with regard to the essentiality of their parts? I therefore have strengthened the two forms of essentialism to cover both actual and merely possible wholes. One might, of course, prefer the Chisholm-Plantinga version if one were sceptical about possible objects but not sceptical about possible states of affairs (since the latter need not involve any objects other than actual objects). It is not my desire to enter into this dispute. Put it this way: if there are any merely possible wholes and parts, then essentialism, if true at all, should be true of them.

Stated as general truths about wholes and parts, both (4*) and (5*) are false. I do not propose to spend much time in arguing against (4*), hological essentialism. Some of the things that Hegel, or various Hegelians, say smack of hological essentialism, but I am not even certain that it would be entirely fair to put (4*) in their mouths, at least in its general and unqualified form. It seems plain that it is possible for the leg of a table to survive the destruction of the table of which it is the leg, and indeed possible that the selfsame leg might have existed without the table ever having existed. When something like hological essentialism has been defended, it has usually been in a more restricted form, as a truth about 'organic' wholes. However, even in this restricted form, it is a mistaken doctrine. The whole is essential to its parts only in the case in which there is some whole x and some part y and some relation R such that it is necessary for y that x stands in relation R to it. In general, even organic examples do not meet this requirement. A heart can exist apart from the animal body in which it functions. Perhaps a hological essentialist could find a way around this sort of counterexample. But what must be incompatible with any reasonable version of hological essentialism, even when restricted to organic examples, is that it be logically possible for there to be a world of hearts but no animal bodies. But surely this is logically possible. Such hearts could not be functioning hearts, at least not functioning in the normal way, and if 'heart' is given a definition that incorporates its normal function, it might then be wrong to call those objects existing in a universe devoid of animal bodies 'hearts'. But those same objects which are hearts in our world could exist in the world devoid of animal bodies, and this shows that hological essentialism is false, even if restricted to organic examples. I do not assert that there are no wholes whatever such that they are necessary for the existence of their parts, but only that, if there be such, in general organic wholes do not provide examples of them.

(5*), mereological essentialism, is perhaps more plausible. Roderick Chisholm, in a paper and in the appendix to a book,[9] argues that mereological essentialism is true. According to Chisholm, mereological essentialism has certain untutored intuitions in its favour. Chisholm sketches what he takes to be a genuine clash between two sorts of intuitions that he thinks we have. On the one hand, he says that we believe such things as that my automobile had parts last week that it does not have this week, and that it will have parts in the future that it never had before. Or that I could have bought different tyres for my automobile from the ones I did buy for it, and if I had done so, then it would have had different tyres than the ones it does have. Let's call these intuitions 'intuitions about the replaceability of parts', or 'replaceability intuitions' for short. The replacements in question are both actual and merely possible ones.

On the other hand, Chisholm asks us to consider a very simple table, made from a stump and a board:

> Now one might have constructed a very similar table by using the same stump and a different board, or by using the same board and a different stump. But the only way of constructing precisely that table is to use that particular stump and that particular board. It would seem, therefore, that that particular table is *necessarily* made up of that particular stump and that particular board.[10]

Let's call these second sort of intuitions 'intuitions about the irreplaceability of parts', or 'irreplaceability intuitions' for short, because Chisholm is not just saying that we believe that objects like tables have necessarily at their origin the parts they in fact have at their origin (but may get new ones subsequently), but rather is saying that we believe that objects have necessarily at all times at which they exist any part they have at any time. The principle of mereological essentialism is then intended to formalise for Chisholm what he thinks is involved in this second sort of intuition. If the principle of mereological essentialism did account for this second sort of intuition, then there would be an apparent inconsistency between the two sets of intuitions, for if parts are essential to the whole, then no part-replacement would be identity-preserving for the whole, and yet the first sort of intuition licensed part-replacement that was identity-preserving for the whole. Chisholm's strategy is to resolve this apparent inconsistency by distinguishing between a loose, popular way of speaking, in which things we are inclined to say while in the grip of replaceability intuitions are true, and a strict, philosophical way of speaking, in which the things we are inclined to say while in the grip of the irreplaceability intuitions are true. Philosophically speaking, mereological essentialism is the truth about wholes and their parts.

I dispute that the correct way in which to account for those cases (like that of the table) in which we have irreplaceability intuitions is by the principle of mereological essentialism, and I therefore deny that there is even an apparent inconsistency between the two sets of intuitions, since they are, after all, intuitions about different cases. The apparent inconsistency only arises if we try to account for the irreplaceability intuitions in the case of the table by the general principle of mereological essentialism, which then must also be true of the automobile, and which would entail that the parts of the automobile are had by the automobile necessarily, and are therefore irreplaceable. Thereby, an apparent inconsistency is generated with the intuitions about the replaceability of the automobile's parts. Our original intuitions told us that the parts of the automobile were replaceable; mereological essentialism tells us that they are not.

But if we can explain our intuitions in the case of the table without adopting the principle of mereological essentialism, then we will have no reason for thinking that the parts of the automobile are irreplaceable, and hence no reason for thinking that any of our beliefs are inconsistent with the belief that the parts of the automobile are replaceable. I think that there is, indeed, another and more plausible explanation for our intuitions in the case of the table than the principle of mereological essentialism, an explanation which will not generate even an apparent inconsistency with our belief about the replaceability of the parts of the automobile.

According to Chisholm, examining our intuitions about the irreplaceability of the parts of the table should get us to see the attractions of the principle of mereological essentialism. I see no such attractions. What I do find attractive is the idea that although some part-replacement is identity-preserving for the whole, there are limits to this. That is, some part-replacement is not identity-preserving for the whole of which they are the parts.

In particular, part-replacement that is either too rapid or too comprehensive or both may not be identity-preserving. A whole can remain numerically the same if some of its parts are replaced in a fell swoop; it can also remain numerically the same if rather more parts are replaced more slowly, over a longer period of time. But a whole may not remain numerically the same if, for example, all or most of its parts are replaced all at once. There are bounds to part-replacement that is identity-preserving for the whole.

Return now to the case of the automobile, which was meant to ground our intuitions about the replaceability of parts. Try to imagine this very same car with every single part replaced in a fell swoop. We would, I think, agree that we would no longer have the same car, since part-replacement of that magnitude is incompatible with the car remaining numerically the same. What we would have obtained thereby is a new car, perhaps qualitatively similar but still numerically distinct from the original car. No one would think that this result should get us to find mereological essentialism attractive, because even if it is essential that a whole not change all its parts at once, it does not follow that there is any part essential to the whole, let alone the stronger proposition that every part is essential to the whole.

The case of the table, which is meant by Chisholm to give rise to intuitions that conflict with our intuitions in the case of the car, is in fact explicable by the very same thought that I cited in the case of the car, i.e. that there are bounds to the part-changes that are identity-preserving for the whole of which they are the parts. In the case of the table, made of only a board and a stump, there is a whole of such relative simplicity that any rapid change of either the complete board or the complete stump is in excess of the limits of identity-preserving part-replacement. That neither stump nor board is really essential to the table can be seen by imagining very gradual replacement of the parts of these parts. Let's say that the wood cells are the parts of both the board and stump. Since the relation of being a part of is transitive, the wood cells are also the parts of the table. Suppose that some of the cells in the board are replaced. Replacement of a few wood cells in the board does not suggest to untutored intuition that the numerical identity of the board or table has been lost. So even in the case of the table, we can imagine some part-replacement (a few wood cells) that is identity-preserving. We can continue replacing wood cells, a few at a time, over a long period, until finally every original wood cell in the board has been changed for a new one. This, too, seems compatible with the numerical identity of the table (and the board too) being retained. It is only massive part-replacement, to wit, the massive number of wood cells that make up the board or stump, done in a fell swoop, that fails to preserve the numerical identity of the table in the case Chisholm imagines. In the case of the table, Chisholm's irreplaceability intuitions about the board and stump are correct, but the explanation for this has nothing to do with a general principle of mereological essentialism.

I do not deny that someone might decide to use the expressions 'whole' and 'part' in such a way that mereo-logical or hological essentialism is true of wholes and parts so-called. My claim is that neither is true of things we normally think of as wholes and parts. What I think Chisholm has done is to confuse aggregates with wholes. Consider this assertion.

(7)   The stars that presently make up the Pleaides galactic cluster occupy an area that measures 700 cubic light years.[11]

Following Tyler Burge, I take the subject of this sentence, and many like it, to be a singular term that refers to an aggregate; in this case, the reference is to an aggregate of stars. The aggregate of stars that presently makes up the cluster is not identical to the cluster itself, and indeed (7) says just this, since it distinguishes between the cluster and the aggregate of stars that presently make it up. At some later time, the cluster might be made up of different stars, and hence a different aggregate of stars, because no change in stars is identity-preserving for the aggregate. In contrast, many star changes can be identity-preserving for the cluster. On the other hand, if the stars fly apart into space, the aggregate of those stars continues to exist if all the stars do, however far-flung and spatially discontinuous from one another the stars might be, whereas the cluster will have ceased to exist.

Aggregates are in some respects like sets, but they are not sets. The aggregate of stars is, like each star, a physical object; the set of stars is an abstract object. No abstract object exists in space, but since (7) gives the spatial dimensions of the subject of (7), the subject must refer to the aggregate of stars rather than to the set of them. Like sets but unlike wholes, aggregates tolerate no identity-preserving changes in constituents, and like sets but unlike wholes, are insensitive to changes in the arrangement or order of those constituents. Other examples of wholes rather like that of a star cluster are the Gulf Stream and the Solar System. One can distinguish between the Gulf Stream and the Solar System on the one hand, and the aggregate(s) of water molecules and naturally orbiting bodies that make up the former and latter respectively at a particular or even at all times.

65

The same distinction can be drawn between ordinary physical objects and the aggregate(s) of microconstituents that make them up at a particular time or at all times. Consider this assertion, analogous to (7):

(8)   The wood cells that presently make up the table occupy an area that measures 2 cubic metres.

I take 'the wood cells that presently make up the table' to be a singular term that refers to an aggregate, the aggregate of wood cells presently making up the table. The table is a whole. The wood cells are among the parts of the table (I say 'among the parts' because the parts of the cells are also parts of the table). Cell replacement is never identity-preserving for the aggregate of wood cells that make up the table at some time, so that now one aggregate of wood cells makes up the table and later another aggregate of wood cells does; every cell replacement is aggregate replacement. But wood cell replacement is often identity-preserving for the table. The table, and indeed the board and the stump, are wholes and not aggregates. Mereological essentialism, a thesis about wholes and parts, is false.

If there is some argument which will show that individuals are not the parts of the social groups to which they belong, that argument will not be sound if it includes as a premiss either (4) or (5). It is in this distinction between wholes and aggregates that I find some truth in (6), that wholes are greater than the sum of their parts. If we give 'sum' the sense of 'aggregate' (or indeed the sense of 'sum' in the calculus of individuals), wholes can survive changes unsurvivable by the sum of their parts. If this is what (6) means, it is true.

Why, though, should wholes and aggregates differ in this way? One difference we have noted is that, unlike wholes, aggregates and sets are insensitive to changes in order or arrangement of constituents. The aggregate and the set of dogs remains numerically the same whether the dogs stand side by side or at a great distance from one another. And, given that they are at a distance from one another, it does not matter, as far as the set or the aggregate is concerned, whether they occupy new positions or even exchange positions with one another. Wholes are not insensitive to arrangement in this way. Thus, one difference between aggregates of parts and sets of parts on the one hand and wholes on the other is that the relations between the parts matter in the case of the latter and do not matter in the case of the former.

Consider some whole, like Chisholm's table. Its parts, the board and the stump, have a certain spatial relation to one another. It is not essential to the continued existence of the table that the board and stump continue in *precisely* the same spatial relation to one another. We can alter that relation to some degree without compromising the existence of the table. What is true about the table, and with other examples of wholes, is that there is often some range of relations, whether spatial or otherwise, such that the parts can stand in any relation to one another in that range, without the identity of the whole being compromised. But that range sets limits such that if the parts stand in relations to one another outside that range, the whole of which they are the parts ceases to exist. For instance, if the stump is put on top of the board, the table ceases to exist.

Having its parts related to one another by some relation from a limited range of possible relations is essential for a whole. This fact helps explain why a whole, unlike an aggregate or set, can remain numerically the same in spite of some part changes. Sameness of relations helps to 'carry' numerical identity across part-changes. Wholes have relations as well as parts to bear the numerical identity through change.

I have stressed the need for the parts of a whole to be related by some relation from a range of possible relations. My example, though, is of a spatial relation. Although most wholes if they exist in space at all, do in fact involve essentially some range of spatial relations between parts, the fundamental requirement for wholes should not require that the relations be spatially restricted in this way; some other range of relations other than spatial relations might play this role. Suppose there were causal action at a distance, and that if a and b were causally related, no change in spatial position of either would alter that causal relation. Suppose there were several parts, $a_1 \ldots a_n$, separated from one another by large expanses of space, or even by other, intervening objects not from the set, $a_1 \ldots a_n$. But finally suppose that $a_1 \ldots a_n$ were causally integrated in such a way that events in any one part caused or were caused by events in other parts, with the consequence that they functioned jointly to achieve some single end. I think that we would have adequate reason to think of $a_1 \ldots a_n$ as the parts of some single whole, in spite of the irrelevance of the spatial relations between the parts. The causal relations between the parts, or a permissible range of such causal relations, could provide what is essential to the whole, in the absence of the relevance of spatial relations.

In the opening remarks of this chapter, I said that I relied on readers' pre-theoretic intuitions about which assemblages of parts constituted a whole and which did not. I said that my belt, your lunch, and Victoria Station did not, even if brought into spatial contact with one another. Even if in fact they are in spatial contiguity to one another, their spatial position relative to one another is of no importance to that assemblage (one can, of course, tell a story such that they *become* important, for example if they become an interesting piece of abstract art). It is the unimportance of any relations between the parts that renders the three items an aggregate but not a whole. In this, I follow Rescher in denying the truth of the mereological principle of universal summability: 'Any two "objects" whatever may be summed; i.e. any pair of "objects" x,y gives rise to an "object" z which is their sum.'[12] I agree with Rescher that: 'There are senses of "part" which do not qualify the sum or join of two parts as a part in turn. . . . Thus, adequate restrictions must be placed on summability.' Universal summability is true for aggregates; any pair of objects x,y gives rise to an aggregate which is their sum. But this is not true for wholes, as the case of my belt, your lunch, and Victoria Station demonstrates, whether or not these items are in spatial contact.

Are individuals the parts of groups: continued

I wish now to return to the chapter's main line of argument. I have argued that mereological and hological essentialism are false. Had they been true, then given what seemed to be some uncontroversial truths about individuals and the groups to which they belong, we might have been able to argue to the conclusion that individuals are not the parts of the groups of which they are the members. Is there some other argument that shows that individuals and groups do not stand in the mereological part-whole relation?

Those who believe that individuals are the parts of the groups to which they belong need not hold that the social relation of being a member of can be analysed as the mereological relation of being a part of. The idea that the social relation of being a member of just *is* the mereological relation of being a part of is false, and this is so not just for the rather obvious reason that some parts, e.g. the parts of a physical object, are not members of that object. Consider the relation of being an s-part of, which is the same relation as the relation of being a part of, except that its range is restricted to social entities. Still, the relation of being a member of could not be identified with the relation of being an s-part of, because the former relation is non-transitive, whereas the latter relation (like the relation of being a part of, from which it is derived) is transitive. If a is an s-part of b, and if b is an s-part of c, then it follows that a is an s-part of c. The membership relation is non-transitive, because I might be a member of a trades union, and the trades union might be a member of the Trades Union Congress, but it might be that no individual can be a member of the TUC. So the membership relation is non-transitive, the mereological relation of being a part of is transitive, and hence these must be different relations, even if the mereological relation were restricted to social applications.

However, the most that those who believe that individuals are the parts of the groups to which they belong need hold is that it follows from the fact that an individual is a member of a group that he is a part of that group. Thus, he needs to hold that, from the fact that some non-transitive relation holds between a person and a group, it follows that some transitive relation also holds between them, and this idea does not seem implausible. Nevertheless, the remainder of this chapter is intended to demonstrate why this idea is false. On my view, from the fact that an individual is a member of a group, it follows that he is *not* a mereological part of that group.

Most writers, including Chisholm, assume without argument that the relation of being a part of is transitive. Rescher, on the other hand, argues that it is not transitive: 'There are various nontransitive senses of "part".'[13] I defend the idea, against Rescher, that the mereological relation of being a part of is transitive. There are two sorts of cases that might make one doubt the transitivity of the part relation. The first case is one that I will only mention now, but deal with more fully later. It is this: 'In military usage . . . persons can be parts of small units, and small units parts of larger ones; but persons are never parts of large units' (Rescher). The way I shall handle this is to deny that persons are ever the parts of the small units to which they belong. The argument confuses the mereological relation of being a part of with the social relation of being a member of or belonging to, and I have already said that the latter relation is non-transitive.

The second sort of case that might lead one to doubt the transitivity of the mereological part relation is this. Suppose that I have an alarm clock, one of whose parts is a light by which one can tell the time in the night. Suppose that I use the clock to make a bomb that detonates when the hands of the clock reach a specified position. The light makes no contribution to the working of the bomb. The light is one of the parts of the clock, and the clock is one of the parts of the bomb, and yet it is false that the light is one of the parts of the bomb. This seems to show that the relation of being a part of is non-transitive.

We need to distinguish between the relations of being one of the parts of and being a part of. The former has, at least in the case of natural organisms and artefacts, functional implications; the latter carries no such implications. Thus, a tumour can be a part of the body without being one of the body's parts. Whatever is one of the parts of something is a part of that thing, but not conversely. The functional relation of being one of the parts of behaves logically very much like the relation of having a function in. A can have a function in b, and b can have a function in c, but a have no function in c. Both the relations of having a function in and being one of the parts of are non-transitive. However, the mereological relation of being a part of is transitive, and it is this relation of being a part of that philosophers write about when they discuss mereology. The light on the alarm clock *is* a part of the bomb, although it is not one of the bomb's parts. Once this distinction is made clear, it does follow that the mereological relation of being a part of will not be adequate on its own for use in biology and other disciplines that require the functional relation.

I wish now to give two arguments, both of whose conclusions will be that no human individuals can be the mereological parts of the groups to which they belong or of which they are the members. These arguments will refute the weak position that asserts that as a matter of contingent fact all members of groups are parts of those groups. *A fortiori*, it refutes the position that it follows from the fact that an individual is a member of some group that he is a part of that group, which is the view that I said earlier that it was the intention of this chapter to refute. The two arguments rely on some further mereological principles about parts and wholes.

Some wholes are abstract objects. Plays, symphonies, novels, and sentences are abstract objects (I am thinking of types, not token performances or inscriptions of these things). These entities are abstract wholes with equally abstract parts – acts, movements, chapters, and words respectively, for example. I have already mentioned these examples in my discussion of the principle of the identity of part-indiscernibles, (3*), for it is these cases which make the principle unsalvageable by means of a temporal qualification.

A necessary but insufficient condition for an object's being abstract is that it is not spatially locatable. The condition is not sufficient, because some mental entities, at least on a dualist analysis, are not spatially locatable either in physical space or in the private space of one's perceptual field, yet they are not abstract entities. I suspect that the a-temporality of an object is both necessary and sufficient for an object's being abstract, and itself grounds the criterion often cited, failure to have causal powers, since (it may be assumed) all causation involves change and nothing not in time can be either changed or a changer.

It follows from the above that I regard not being spatially locatable as a necessary but insufficient condition for not being temporally locatable. Beyond this, I am unclear about how temporality and spatiality relate to one another, or indeed whether they can be fully distinguished (I am thinking of space-time). I sidestep all such problems; for my purposes here, I concentrate on the a-spatiality of abstract objects alone.

The following principle, I claim, is true:

(9)   If x is a whole and if $a_1 \ldots a_n$ are all of its parts, then if $a_1 \ldots a_n$ have no spatial location, x has no spatial location.

As I argued in the case of (2), (9) is not *ad hoc*. The idea that motivates them and gives them their plausibility is that the whole must have the spatial features had by the parts. Some properties of parts do not carry over to be the property of the whole with those parts. But various spatial character-istics are not like that. (9) says that the property of having no spatial location is not like that. If the proper parts of a whole have that property, having no spatial location, then the whole with those parts has that property too – i.e. it has no spatial location. How could one take non-spatial parts and put them together, in such a way as to obtain a whole with spatial location?

(2) asserted that the property of having a spatial location similarly 'carried over' from parts to whole. (2) stated that if the parts have a spatial location, the whole which has those parts has a spatial location too. However, we must distinguish between two different types of spatially locatable items: material entities and certain non-material (in part-icular social) entities. I have in mind a distinction drawn by David Armstrong between 'concrete' and 'abstract' part-iculars, although I prefer my terms, 'material' and 'non-material' (and substitute these expressions for his in the following quote) in order to avoid confusing these two

different types of space-occupying entities with abstract entities in the sense 'do not occupy space at all': 'While it is true that only one [material] particular can have the one total position, this does not hold for [non-material but spatially locatable] particulars'.[14] Armstrong's own example of non-material but spatially locatable entities are a visual cube and a tactile cube, both 'parts' (his word) of a coloured, physical cube. I think that better examples of spatially locatable, non-material entities are some social entities. An example of such entities, akin to an example I mentioned in chapter 1, is this: France might easily have the same spatial boundaries as some other social entity. Suppose for instance that the Catholic Church divided the world into super-dioceses, and one of them, Prance, happened to coincide in area with France. Indeed, France and Prance could have spatially coincident parts. The parts of France are departments; the parts of Prance might be normal dioceses. It could happen that each department perfectly coincided with some diocese.

Materiality and non-materiality link up with spatial properties in this way: as David Wiggins puts it, 'material things have to compete for room in the world'.[15] That is,

(10)   If two entities a and b are material, and if a and b
        are either parts or wholes, then a and b cannot
        both completely occupy the same total position at
        the same time.

It is necessary to include the condition that both a and b are either a part or a whole, in order to exclude the case in which one of them is an aggregate. Suppose material parts $a_1 \ldots a_n$ make up a material whole, x. Both x, and the aggregate of $a_1 \ldots a_n$, are material, and both completely occupy at the same time the same total spatial position.

It would be neat if the converse of (10) were true, but I have my doubts about this. If we know of two entities that they cannot both completely occupy the same total position at the same time, and that neither is an aggregate, can we conclude that they are material? Some argue that a state is the supreme power or authority in a certain area or location, such that if each of two competing authorities share power in a manner not sanctioned by the other, neither constitutes the state. If this is so, it would follow that two states, even though they are intuitively non-material, cannot occupy the same total position at the same time.

We do not need to make up our minds about this case, and hence about the truth of the converse of (10). We know that some social entities, like France and Prance, do not compete for room in the world, and hence can both completely occupy the same total position at the same time. This is sufficient to permit us to conclude, by contraposition, that either France or Prance or both are non-material but spatially locatable. There are many puzzling metaphysical questions about these non-material but spatially locatable entities. For instance, it might be held that there are logically possible worlds with abstract but no material objects. Are there logically possible worlds with non-material spatially locatable objects but no material objects? There are other grounds for thinking it impossible that there be any social entities without there being any individuals, but, aside from this point, are there further reasons for thinking that the existence of any entity of the type, non-material but spatially locatable, logically presupposes some entity of the type, material? I think that there must be reasons for holding that non-material but spatially locatable entities are parasitic on material entities. One such reason would be the idea that a notion of public space presupposed material particulars.[16]

Individuals are not the parts of the groups to which they belong: first argument

The first argument I wish to offer, whose conclusion is that individuals are not the mereological parts of the groups to which they belong, relies on these two additional mereological principles:

(11) If x is a whole and if $a_1 \ldots a_n$ are all of its parts, then if $a_1 \ldots a_n$ are material, x is material.

(12) If x is a whole and if $a_1 \ldots a_n$ are all of its parts, then if $a_1 \ldots a_n$ are spatially locatable but non-material, then x is spatially locatable but non-material.

74

Again, as in the case of (2) and (9), there is nothing *ad hoc* about (11) and (12). The thought behind them, as in the case of the others, is that some spatial characteristics, here the connected feature of materiality or non-materiality, of the parts carry over to the whole with those parts. (11) says, roughly, that material parts put together yield a material whole (if they yield any whole). (12) says, roughly, that non-material but spatially locatable parts put together yield a non-material but spatially locatable whole (if they yield any whole). In both (11) and (12), I mean by 'space' physical space. I think that (12) is true when about the private space of the perceptual field as well, and although I am not here interested in this latter application, it might be applicable in Gestalt psychology.[17]

Do groups have spatial position? If not, human beings, entities which uncontroversially have a spatial location (at least at some times even if not at all times), cannot be the parts of groups, by (2). (2) said that if the parts have spatial location, then the whole with those parts has spatial location. So let's assume that groups do have a spatial location (this sounds right in any case), and indeed have the spatial location of their members.

Two groups can and sometimes do have identical memberships. For instance, all and only the members of some ruling class might be the members of some caste, or all and only the members of some large family might be the members of some theatrical troupe. Both of these things do sometimes occur, but the argument relies only on the fact that these are possible states of affairs. Now, given the possibility of identical memberships, if groups do have the spatial location of their members, it must then be possible for two or more groups to completely occupy the same total position at the same time. That is, the total spatial position of one group can be identical with the total position of another group at the same time. Since two groups can do this, it follows by the contraposition of (10) that either one or both of the groups is non-material. But since both entities are groups, are of the same type, there is no reason to say that one but not the other is material. Neither is material, and indeed neither excludes some material entity from completely occupying the same total position at the same time (e.g., some geophysical tract of land). If we substitute 'some human individuals' for '$a_1 \ldots a_n$' and 'some group' for 'x' in (11), we obtain:

(11*)   If some group is a whole and if there are some individuals who are its parts, then if the individuals are material, the group is material.

The consequent of (11*) is false, as we know from the conjunction of (10), the possibility that two groups have identical membership, and the ascription of the spatial location of a group from the spatial location of its members. But since individuals are material – although a very special sort of material entity – it follows that either the group is no whole (has no parts), or that, although it has parts, the human individuals who belong to it are not among them.

David Wiggins claims[18] that this is a true principle:

(S*)   No two things of the same kind (that is, no two things which satisfy the same sortal or substance concept) can occupy exactly the same volume at exactly the same time.

I am not certain that I disagree with (S*), because I am not certain how Wiggins wishes us to take 'sortal or substance concept'. Elsewhere[19] he says that he intends 'sortal concept' roughly in the sense used by Strawson in the second part of *Individuals*, and there Strawson assumes that all universals are either sortal or characterising universals. This would suggest that the concept of a group is a sortal concept (presumably, 'It presupposes no antecedent principle, or method, of individuating the particulars it collects'[20]), and so if groups do occupy space, (S*) is false of them. Since every group is a group, there are two things of the same kind that can occupy exactly the same volume at the same time.

Individuals are not the parts of the groups to which they belong: second argument

Two further mereological principles that are true are these:

(13) If $a_1 \ldots a_n$ are material parts, then they can just completely compose one whole at a time at most.

(14) If $a_1 \ldots a_n$ are spatially locatable but non-material parts, they can just completely compose one whole at a time at most.

On the other hand, this is false:

(15) If $a_1 \ldots a_n$ are abstract parts, then they can just completely compose one whole at a time at most.

We have already seen that (15) is false, and explained the falsity of (3*), even with a temporal qualification, by in effect assuming the falsity of (15). Precisely the same notes or words can, simultaneously, be used to compose two different tunes or poems, by structuring the same notes or words in different ways.

Some of the terms of (13) and (14) need clarification. Of course, some set of material parts, for instance, might fail to compose *any* whole at a time, either because they are insufficient to make a whole, or because the parts, although in themselves sufficient, are not related in the appropriate way. An example of the former would be my heart, kidneys, and liver, positioned relative to one another as they are in my body, but which on their own are insufficient to compose any whole. An example of the latter would be all the parts of my body, strewn across a battlefield.

I add 'just', because the parts of my body plus the parts of your body do completely compose more than one whole at a time, but they do not *just* do so, since something less than the conjoined parts completely composes a whole, namely the parts of my body alone. Finally, the parts of a clock might just completely compose a clock, and also help to compose a bomb, if the clock is a part of the bomb. But the parts of the clock cannot just *completely* compose more than the clock at one time.

Since human beings are material objects of a certain kind,

my argument relies *only* on (13). However, I wish to defend (14) as well, in the light of a possible counterexample. Suppose that, by appropriate withdrawals and additions to membership, the very same countries were members of both NATO and the International Monetary Fund. Would we not then have some social entities, nations, which were just able to completely compose two social wholes at the same time, NATO and the IMF? We have already admitted that it is possible for a whole to have its parts separated from one another by entities not themselves among its parts, so we are not entitled to deny that NATO and the IMF are wholes on those grounds.

Still, I claim that this does not constitute a counterexample to (14), because the IMF and NATO are not mereological wholes whose parts are the member states. My reason for this denial is as follows. It is uncontroversially true that Macedonia is a mereological part of Greece. Suppose Greece were a part of the IMF. It is false that Macedonia is a mereological part of the IMF. What this shows is that if we say that Greece is part of the IMF, we are using the term 'is a part of' to assert that the relation of being a member of holds between Greece and the IMF, a non-transitive relation, and *not* to assert that the transitive mereological relation of being a part of holds between them. If this explanation were not correct, we should have to accept the patently false conclusion that Macedonia was a mereological part of the IMF.

Similarly, in the example of the same nations forming NATO and the IMF, the nations are the members of, but not the mereological parts of, both NATO and the IMF. I concede, of course, that the very same members can just completely constitute the full membership of more than one social entity (organisation, association, club, or whatever) at a time. I do not admit that (14) is false, that the same social parts, in the mereological sense, can just completely compose more than one social whole at a time.

Nor do I permit these examples to defeat the transitivity claim for the mereological part relation. In Rescher's example, that I cited earlier, persons can be the parts of small military units, and small military units the parts of large military units, but persons might not be the parts of those larger military units. Just as I denied that Greece was a mereological part of the IMF (Greece belongs to the IMF), so too would I deny that persons are the mereological parts of the small units to which they belong. As I remarked in the opening paragraphs of this chapter, I do not dispute that we use the words 'part', 'is a part of', and so on in these cases, and that we do so properly. What I claim is that we sometimes use these words and expressions to indicate something other than the holding of the mereological relation of being a part of, and this is precisely what we are doing in the cases now before us. Careful attention to the difference between the membership relation and the part relation renders, I claim, all similar alleged counterexamples to the transitivity claim for the part relation ineffective.

The second argument for the conclusion that individuals are not the mereological parts of the groups to which they belong relies on the same fact as did the first argument: two or more groups can have precisely the same members at the same time. This fact, together with (13), shows that the individuals cannot be the mereological parts of two or more groups which have the same membership. Individuals are material, and thus at a time can just completely compose one whole at most. If those individuals simultaneously constitute the complete membership of two groups, they could at most be the parts of one of the groups.

We can extend the argument. Suppose someone argued either (a) that in the case of two or more groups with identical memberships, the individuals were the parts of only one of the groups, or (b) that in the case of groups which did not have identical memberships, there was no barrier to saying that their members were their parts. Both (a) and (b) have at least two things wrong with them. First, they are entirely under-motivated. There is no reason to think that there are the metaphysical differences between groups in the way in which they imply. Second, the claims would find it difficult to account for what went on, metaphysically speaking, in certain membership changes. Suppose there were two groups, x and y, with identical members, and that the members were the parts of x but not y.

Suppose further that there is a membership change so that the memberships are no longer identical. Do the individuals then become the parts of y as well as x? Or, suppose there were two groups, x and y, with different memberships and hence such that the members of both were their parts. Suppose further that the memberships of x and y become identical. Do the members then cease to be the parts of either x or y? If so, of which? I conclude, therefore, that the individual members are the parts of no groups.

The intuitive plausibility of (11), (12), (13) and (14) is strengthened by noting that there are some genuine wholes of which individuals are the bona fide mereological parts, and that all four principles are true of these cases. Consider those formations and configurations (a pyramid, for instance) that acrobats in a circus can get themselves into by standing on or being otherwise supported by one another. Or, consider lines or rows of people, or queues at a bus stop, or crowds or mobs of people. These are all material entities which simultaneously exclude any other material entity from simultaneously occupying completely the same total position.

These material entities are the wholes formed from human beings as parts, themselves material entities. This is what our principles would lead us to expect: put material parts together, and a material whole will result. Moreover, if human beings $a_1 \ldots a_n$ are the parts of the line, then there is no other whole of which they can simultaneously just be all the parts.

The four principles reveal some of the important differences between the mereological relation of being a part of and the social relation of being a member of. The two arguments I have given that make use of (some of) these principles give us conclusive reason to refuse to conflate the mereological relation of being a part of with the social relation of being a member of, and in particular to refuse to count the members of social entities of any sort as their parts. If the queue waiting for a 38 bus forms itself into local branch 38 of the bus-users' association, the individuals in the queue are the parts, not the members, of the queue, and are the members, not the parts, of the local branch of the bus-users' association. Each of the individuals in the queue is a material entity and so is the queue that they make up. No material entity can completely occupy the same total spatial position occupied by the queue at the same time, unless it is just identical with the queue. On the other hand, the local association of bus-users is a social entity, and if it did have parts, perhaps committees, they would also be social entities. Some other entity can completely occupy precisely the same total spatial position at the same time, if indeed an association of this sort has any spatial position at all, for the same individuals might form themselves into any number of analogous associations they care to create.

Minds and mereology

Persons are either (a) mental entities, either in an embodied or disembodied state, or (b) material entities, or (c) complexes of a mental and a material entity. In this chapter, at various points quite essential to my argument, I have asserted that individuals have spatial location, and that they are material entities, perhaps of a special sort. These remarks are consistent with the second and third alternatives I have mentioned, but hardly consistent with the first. If persons are minds, then they never have spatial location, not even when they are embodied (although of course their bodies have a spatial location.

Perhaps the reader will think that it is no great matter that my remarks are inconsistent with (a). The trouble with this is that I take great pains in chapter 3 to avoid commitment concerning what it is to be a person. I intend my analysis of the social in chapter 3 to permit the possibility of a society of disembodied minds (assuming of course that a disembodied mind is itself a logical possibility). Part of my motive for this is that I know of no sound argument with non-question-begging premises, whose conclusion is that a disembodied person is a logical impossibility. If there could be disembodied persons, I cannot see anything logically absurd in the idea that there could be social relations between them.

81

So it would seem that none of my arguments in this chapter could show that disembodied minds cannot be the mereological parts of the social groups to which they might belong, as long as those groups too had no spatial location. In fact, my difficulty is more acute than that. If persons are mental entities, I have no argument to show that they cannot be the mereological parts of non-spatially locatable social entities, even when the persons are embodied! Suppose that persons are minds, but that for certain periods of their existence (this might include the whole of their existence) they exist in an embodied state. Even so, it might be held that even in those periods of embodiment, it is the persons as mental entities, and not their bodies, which are the mereological parts of the (non-spatially locatable) groups, or other social entities, to which they belong. No mereological principle that I have thus far used in this chapter will rule this possibility out.

The problem with this apparent possibility is that I do not find myself with any clear intuitions about how the mereological language of 'part' and 'whole' might apply in the case of minds and wholes (whatever they might be) of which individual minds would be the mereological parts. I cannot see any way to dismiss the suggestion that social groups are the wholes of which individual minds are the parts, nor can I see any way in which the suggestion might be supported. The possibility we are meant to evaluate asks us to take our mereological language and apply it to a case which stretches it beyond a point at which we have any clear ideas about how to assess the plausibility of its use. One may of course *stipulate* that minds are the mereological parts of social groups, but one should also show, if one does this, what reasons there are for this stipulation.

More fruitfully, I hope, I turn in chapter 3 to an analysis of the social, and it is there where we shall see with what justification one might speak of social relations between disembodied minds (if it is logically possible that there be disembodied minds).

CHAPTER 3

Social properties and their basis

In the first two chapters, I have been concerned with questions about social entities. In the first chapter, I argued that there are good reasons for thinking that e-holism (the view that there are some irreducible social entities) is true. In chapter 2, I described some metaphysical truths about those entities. Hitherto, I have had nothing to say about p-holism (the view that there are some irreducible social properties), other than merely distinguishing it from e-holism. The intent of this chapter is to make good that omission.

There is an old Russian proverb, quoted in Vladimir Medem's autobiography, that says: 'An individual in Russia was composed of three parts: a body, a soul, and a passport.' Although the saying speaks of three kinds of entities, I shall speak of three kinds of properties: material, mental, and social. I do not think that these three types of properties are exhaustive of the types of properties that there are. For example, I think that there are moral and mathematical properties. But these three are the only types of properties that will concern me in this chapter.

Except in the case of social properties, I rely on readers' intuitions about which specific properties are of one or another kind, and why this might be so. Having such-and-such mass is a material property; desiring something is a mental property; voting and purchasing are social properties. It is not my intention to discuss, or to beg any questions about, the relation between mental and material properties. The question of social properties is more than enough to deal with here. In what follows, I speak of material and mental properties as if these were different kinds of properties. For those who think that material and mental properties are irreducibly different, my terminology will pose no difficulty. But my way of speaking is meant only as a terminological convenience, not as the result of a philosophical decision. For those who think that mental properties are a species of material property, let them in what follows read the contrast between mental and material properties as a contrast between a specific subset of material properties and all the other material properties not in that subset. Indeed, if there are those who think that material properties are a species of mental property, let them in what follows read the contrast between material and mental properties as a contrast between a specific subset of mental properties and all the other mental properties not in that subset. Nothing whatever hangs on this in what follows.

I have spoken, especially in chapter 1, of various ontological doctrines as either holistic or individualistic. The former denies that a certain reductive identification is possible, the latter asserts that it is. Since these are doctrines about reductive identification, they are relational theses – about social entities or properties, and some (other) kind of entities or properties, with which the former can or cannot be reductively identified. Which (other) kind of entities or properties? Characterising holism poses no special problems in this regard, since it is the thesis that social entities or social properties are irreducible to entities or properties of *any* other kind. Of course, there may be difficulties in elucidating what is to count as a *kind* of entity or property for metaphysical purposes, but once this is done, there is no further difficulty involved in stating holism. But individualism has an added difficulty. It must specify with which kind of property or entity social properties or social entities can be reductively identified. What *kind* of individuals is individualism about?

I assume that the individuals in question, which give individualism its rationale, are either material entities or properties, or mental entities or properties, or mixes of both material and mental entities or properties. Thus, e-individualism asserts that social entities can be reduced to material or mental entities or mixes thereof. In chapter 1 I spoke, *inter alia*, of human beings as the candidate for reducing entity. Metaphysically speaking, it does not matter, as far as individualism is concerned, whether we construe human beings as material entities, or as embodied mental entities, or as unique composites of the two types of entities. Similarly, p-individualism asserts that social properties can be reductively identified with material properties, or with mental properties, or with disjunctions thereof.

Chapter 2 indicated a reason why holism is so badly named (because social entities are not wholes whose parts are individual persons). Individualism is also badly named – because it gives no clue as to the metaphysical type to which the individuals in question belong. One could more illuminatingly speak about materialism or mentalism with regard to the social, just as we speak of materialism with regard to issues about the mental. Or perhaps better still, we could argue in terms of sociopsychological or sociophysical monism.

Since I limit my sights to the material, the mental, and the social, it will be sufficient, in order to demonstrate the irreducibility of social properties, to demonstrate their irreducibility to material and mental properties. In fact, my main effort will go into showing their irreducibility to the mental, for I do not think it would be plausible to hold that their reduction to the material alone could be adequate. That is, there are properties which we take to be mental properties, and even if we eventually construe those properties as material properties of a special sort, no reduction of social properties will be successful unless it *at least includes* properties of that kind.

The question I wish to answer then is this: Can social properties be reductively identified with mental properties (perhaps in combination with material properties)? The thought may seem plausible that they can be so reductively identified. What is it, after all, to be an alderman, or a mayor, or an army officer, but for certain beliefs and attitudes to be generally true? Where shall we understand the social to be but in the realm of the mind? Of course, the beliefs and attitudes must be widely held, for a person's believing that he is an army officer does not make him one. But there is certainly some sort of affinity between the social and the mental, and might it not be that being an army officer can be understood as a general system of beliefs and attitudes widely held? Isn't the reality of the social character- istics of persons connected with the ways in which they think about and consider each other? Isn't the reality of the social characteristics of things connected with the ways in which they are thought about by persons?

In the course of the chapter, I offer reasons for thinking that the identification (if there is one) of a social property of a particularly characteristic type with mental properties would be circular, and hence not reductive, in the sense that I gave to this sort of charge in chapter one. I take myself to have offered, in this chapter, reasons for thinking that social properties of that sort are irreducible to mental properties and to combinations or mixes of mental and material properties. It would be too strong to say that I demonstrate irreducibility on grounds of circularity, but I think I offer reasons for believing that this is so.

The categories of the material, mental, and social

It would be useful to have some sort of clear classificatory scheme for the predicability of the categories of the material, mental, and social, even if there is some element of arbitrariness in the choice of scheme. I first discuss whether an entity can have properties of more than one type. I then employ the classificatory scheme which I adopt to examine the question of whether the conjunction of e-holism and p-individualism could be true. Since I accept that there is a certain measure of arbitrariness in my choice of classificatory scheme, to that extent I admit a degree of arbitrariness in my claim that the conjunction of the two views is logically

86

inconsistent. Still, I think that my choice of classificatory scheme is intuitively appealing, and that there is a lot that may be said in its favour. I now proceed to say it.

First, let us see what kinds of properties appear to be predicable of what kinds of entities. The simplest case seems to be that of irreducibly social entities. If an entity (a nation or group, for example) is irreducibly social, then no mental or material property is true of it. Thus, irreducibly social entities like groups and nations do not have beliefs and desires. If they have interests, then the having of interests is not a mental property (this conclusion seems right on independent grounds). As for material properties, no genuinely material property can be true of, for example, France or the McAdam clan. I agree that these entities may be situated in physical space, and that various persons, themselves material entities, may belong to them. But I hope that I have said enough in chapter 2 to make it clear why neither the property of being situated in physical space nor the property of having persons as members is itself a material or physical property. I believe that the property of having material mereological parts is a material property, but that no nation or group has this property. I believe that having (material) individuals as members is a property had by nations and groups, but that this is a social rather than a material property. In denying that there are any irreducible social entities, what the e-individualist denies is the existence of entities with irreducible social properties but no mental or material properties. It is this e-individualist view against which I have argued in both of the preceding chapters.

If an entity is irreducibly mental, then no material property can be true of it. But, as I shall say later more fully, there could be social properties true of minds. I cannot see that there is any logical impossibility in the idea, assuming that there could be disembodied minds, that these minds could be socially related. For example, disembodied minds might co-exist in a Kantian Kingdom of Ends, or – less grandiosely – might form themselves into groups. So irreducibly mental entities may have social properties true of them.

If an entity is irreducibly material, both mental and social properties may be true of it. For instance, those who believe that token brain state-mental state identity is logically possible but that the corresponding type-type identity theory is false believe that it is logically possible that there are material things of which mental properties are true. On some accounts of what it is to be a person, persons are material entities of which some mental properties are also true. As for irreducibly material entities of which some social properties are true, pound notes, credit cards, and aldermen provide examples. A credit card is a material thing, a bit of plastic, of which certain social properties, like usability in purchase, are true. If a person is a material entity, then an alderman is a material entity, of whom a social property, like the property of having been elected by some procedure, is true. The properties in these examples are all social properties true of material entities, not of social entities.

In sum, if an entity is irreducibly social, then no material or mental property can be true of it. If an entity is irreducibly mental, then no material property can be true of it but some social properties can be true of it. If an entity is irreducibly material, both social and mental properties can be true of it.

P-individualism and e-holism

An e-holist asserts that there are some irreducible social entities. The p-holist asserts that there are some irreducible social properties. The p-holist who is an e-individualist believes that all the irreducible social properties that there are, are true only of either material or mental entities. They cannot be true of social entities, of the irreducible kind, because there aren't any.

In chapter 1, I said that p-holism might be true even if e-holism were false (this is the doctrine I have just described in the preceding paragraph). I was non-committal about the possibility of e-holism being true even if p-holism were false, beyond saying that the doctrine was not very attractive. Perhaps more can now be said about this.

What would the supposition that e-holism is true but p-holism false entail? E-holism asserts the existence of irreducible social entities. It follows that neither mental nor material properties can be true of such entities. Let's assume (what is surely true) that every entity must have some property. What properties would these irreducible social entities have, if neither material nor mental ones? P-individualism asserts that there are no irreducible social properties, so it follows that they can have none of these either. We seem to be presented with a dilemma: either these irreducible social entities have social properties which are reducible, or they have no social properties at all, whether reducible or irreducible.

Consider the first horn of the dilemma: these irreducible social entities have reducible social properties. What kind of properties are these reducible social properties reducible to? They cannot be reducible to material or to mental properties, since we have already agreed that if an entity is irreducibly social, then no material or mental property can be true of it. Although I have not demonstrated that there are no other kinds of properties to which social properties could be reduced (moral or mathematical properties, for instance), the thought is sufficiently implausible to warrant no further discussion.

The second horn holds that these irreducible social entities have no social properties at all, neither reducible nor irreducible social properties. Against this possibility, we might ask why such entities counted as irreducible social entities at all. I said earlier that if an entity is an irreducible social entity, it followed that no material or mental property is true of it. I did not add that it followed that some social property is true of it (nor did I say that if an entity is irreducibly mental or material, then some mental or material property, respectively, *must* be true of it). But surely we are entitled to add just this. How could a wedge be placed between, on the one hand, possession by an entity of the metaphysical property of being an entity belonging to some metaphysical kind, and, on the other hand, possession by that entity of some specific properties of that kind? Being an entity of some metaphysical kind (being a material entity, being a mental entity, being a social entity, being an abstract entity) is not a basic, non-consequential property of an entity. It is a supervenient property of an entity, which that entity possesses as a consequence of possessing some specific properties belonging to that kind (e.g. having such-and-such atomic weight, being felt intensely, being a charter member of the United Nations, being the smallest prime number).

Thus, an entity is an irreducible social entity only if it has at least one social property true of it. Every irreducible social entity (every reducible social entity, too, but we need only the weaker claim for the argument at hand) must have some social property true of it. Similarly for mental and material entitites. Every irreducible material entity must have some material property true of it. Every irreducible mental entity must have some mental property true of it.

Thus, there cannot be an irreducible social entity with no social property true of it at all. Being a social entity is a metaphysical property true of entities only if those entities have some specific social property (this is a necessary but insufficient condition for an entity being a social entity). We dismissed the first horn of the dilemma, that irreducible social entities have only reducible social properties. We can also now dismiss the second horn of the dilemma, that these irreducible social entities have no social properties whatever, whether reducible or irreducible. It follows, considering both horns, that they must have some social properties, and that not all of those social properties can be *reducible* social properties. Neither horn of the dilemma is possible. So, if there are irreducible social entities and if every entity must possess some property, p-individualism must be false. If an entity is an irreducible social entity, it follows that it has at least one irreducible social property true of it.

If the above argument is sound, it means that if e-holism is true, it follows that p-holism is true (with the addition of some suitable but plausible premises). So, in a sense, the argument of this chapter is supererogatory. If I had succeeded in chapter 1 in demonstrating the truth of e-holism, then it follows that I would have demonstrated the truth of p-holism. But it would surely be philosophically unwise to pursue this strategy. First, I admitted in several places in chapter 1 that I could not demonstrate that my argument was sound; I said that, at best, I could show that there were good reasons for thinking that the conclusion of my argument, that there are some irreducible social entities, was true. Second, even in my argument above, in which I argue for the link between p-holism and e-holism, there is perhaps the possibility of rejoinder (e.g. even if possession of the metaphysical property of being an entity of a specific metaphysical kind is a consequential property, why must it be possessed in consequence of possession of specific properties of that kind? Why not just in consequence of possession of other metaphysical properties?). Third, there is a certain element of arbitrariness, to which I have already admitted, in my choice of classificatory scheme, and my argument above makes essential use of that scheme of classification. Fourth, and finally, there is a general diffidence one ought always to feel about one's philosophical argument – induction ought to lead one to expect that someone is bound to find some fault with it, in spite of the fact that that fault is not apparent to him who produces the argument. In this chapter, then, I attempt to argue directly for p-holism, without relying on the fact that it follows from e-holism, conjoined with some additional but plausible premises. There is no harm in this. At best, I will have given two independent, sound arguments for the same conclusion.

The reducibility of social properties: the criterion for property identity

As I have already asserted, if social properties were reducible, the obvious and plausible candidates would be either mental properties or mixes of both material and mental properties. Suppose, then, that someone were to claim that some social property S = some mental or material property M, or that some social property S = some disjunction of material or mental properties $M_1 \ldots M_n$. I express myself thus, in order to avoid assuming that a disjunction of properties is itself a property. I wish to make my remarks *consistent* with the view, stated by D.M. Armstrong and others, that a disjunction of properties may not itself be a property.[1] For those who think that a disjunction of properties is itself a property, the first clause of the above supposition is sufficient. I wish to make my remarks consistent with Armstrong's thesis, in order to avoid what I take to be an irrelevant reply to what I have to say.

What in general must be true for a property S to be identical with some property, or disjunction of properties, M? It is uncontroversial that this condition is too weak: $(x)(Sx \equiv Mx)$. Extensional equivalence is too weak, because if it were sufficient, it would be trivially easy to show that for each social property S, there is some material or mental property M, or disjunction of such material or mental properties, with which it is identical.

Here is my argument for this assertion. Consider the social property of being a mayor, and consider the set of all the mayors there ever have been or ever will be. It is certainly true that no one is now in a position to say who is in that set and who is not. Such epistemic difficulties notwithstanding, there must still *be* such a set, the set of all and only those individuals who are mayors at any time.

For each mayor in the set, there is bound to be some material or mental identifying description true only of him or her. I say 'bound to be', because I do not wish to rest my argument on some supposedly logically necessary truth that it is impossible that there be a world in which there are two indiscernible non-identicals (indeed, I think it possible for there to be such a world, either if it is spatially symmetrical, or if it contains two non-spatially related spaces). Rather, what we are considering here is the criterion of extensional equivalence for property identity, and I am posing the actuality, not the logical necessity, that there is for every mayor some material or mental property (or mix thereof) that uniquely discerns him from everything else. In fact, my argument relies on something even weaker than the claim that as a matter of fact there is some material or mental property that uniquely discerns him from everything else: the weaker claim that I need is that there is in fact at least

92

one such property true of each mayor and of nothing that fails to be a mayor. In virtue of some material or mental property, each mayor can be distinguished from every non-mayor. It would not trouble my argument if there were two or more mayors indiscernible from each other on material and mental grounds. But this is so implausible that I continue to use the unnecessarily stronger claim: as a matter of fact (but not of logical necessity), there is for each mayor at least one material or mental property or disjunction thereof true of that mayor and nothing else whatever. This is an assumption, but a very weak and surely factually correct one.

Now, if it is true that for each mayor there is some material or mental property true of that mayor and nothing else, then it follows that there must be some complex disjunctive material or mental property, or mix thereof (or some disjunction of material or mental properties, or mix thereof, if disjunctions of properties are not themselves properties), with each disjunct true of a mayor and nothing else, and such that each mayor has at least one of the disjuncts true of him. So the complex property (or the disjunction of properties) must be true of all and only the mayors that there are. Call this complex disjunctive property (or disjunction) 'M'. Call the social property of being a mayor 'S'. S is true of all and only those things of which M is true, which is to say that they are extensionally equivalent. Even if we cannot now specify those material or mental properties, or formulate any rule for generating them, we can now know a priori (but modulo the assumption that there is in fact some material or mental property true of each mayor and nothing else) that there must be such properties M and S which are extensionally equivalent. If identificatory victory were to be bought this cheaply, the right conclusion must be that extensional equivalence is too weak a condition for property identity.

The weakest plausible criterion for property identity that I know is necessary co-extensiveness, where the necessity involved might arguably be either nomological or logical. Thus, we might say that property S = property M iff $N(x)(Sx \equiv Mx)$, where 'N' represents the operator for either logical or nomological necessity. I conduct the following discussion in terms of nomological rather than logical necessity only because it is the weaker of the two ideas. Nothing in what follows presupposes the readers' acceptance of the idea of nomological or physical necessity. I introduce it only to examine and dismiss arguments which rely on that idea.[2] So the question that now confronts us is: are there any material or mental properties or disjunctions thereof which are logically or nomologically necessary and sufficient for each (or, any) social property?

The reducibility of properties: the argument from alternative realisations

There is in the literature an argument which alleges to show that no material property could be nomologically necessary and sufficient for any mental property. The argument is standardly used against type-type psychophysical identity theories. It might repay us to examine that argument, for if it were sound, we might be able to export it from the philosophy of mind and apply it to the question of the reduction of social to material/mental properties. Let's call this sort of argument 'an argument from alternative realisations'. Various authors, such as Hilary Putnam, Jaegwon Kim and Colin McGinn, as well as other philosophers who defend 'functionalism' in the philosophy of mind, have used some variation of the basic idea of alternative realisations.[3] The argument, or argument-sketch, I set out below is a reconstruction, which I hope is fair to the intentions of those who espouse this type of argument and presents the argument in a promising form, although no author of whom I am aware sets out his argument in just this way. I here designate material properties by 'M' and mental properties by 'E' (in the preceding sections I have used 'M' to designate both material and mental properties, since I was there only interested in the contrast of both of them with social properties).

(A)   For any material property M and any mental property

E, if M = E, then $N(x)(Mx \equiv Ex)$.

(B) Suppose there is some M which is nomologically sufficient for E.

(C) For any such M, it is nomologically possible that there is an x which is E but not M.

(D) Hence no M which is nomologically sufficient for E is also nomologically necessary for E.

(E) Therefore, it is false for any E and M that $N(x)(Mx \equiv Ex)$.

(F) Therefore, it is false for any E and M that E = M.

Those who put forward this sort of argument do not deny that there are material properties which are nomologically sufficient for mental properties, in the sense that, in virtue of a law of nature, anything which has that material property true of it must have that mental property true of it. Those who put forward this sort of argument and who deny that there is a relation of identity between any material and any mental property often say that another relation, that of supervenience, holds between material and mental properties, and as far as I can understand the idea of supervenience, it presupposes that for every mental property there is some material property or properties nomologically sufficient for it.

Presumably, supporters of this argument need not deny either that there are some material properties which are nomologically necessary for mental properties – for example, it might be necessary in virtue of a law of nature that any being in some mental state could not be composed only of liquid iodine and californium. What the supporters of this argument deny is that there is any material property that is both nomologically necessary and nomologically sufficient for any mental property. Sometimes the argument is illustrated with examples of artefacts such as clocks and their alternative physical realisations: 'we shall not expect the physical realisations of artefacts, e.g. clocks, we have not observed to conform by natural necessity to those we have.'[4] That is, we should not expect the sort of physical realisations of observed clocks to be nomologically necessary for unobserved clocks. Similarly, we should not expect the sort of material realisations of mental properties that we have observed to be nomologically necessary for all creatures, observed and unobserved, of whom the mental property is or may be true.

One problem that arises is how we can know that premises like (C) and (D) are true. McGinn thinks that these premises are knowable a priori: 'what is a priori . . . is that [such extensional equivalences as there might be] are not lawlike'.[5] Hilary Putnam, on the other hand, takes premises like (C) and (D), whether concerning material-artefact property identity or material-mental property identity, to be knowable only a posteriori. In the main, he asserts that we *now* know that such premises are true: 'For we already know that such laws would be false . . . because even in the light of our present knowledge we can see that any Turing Machine that can be physically realised at all can be realised in a host of totally different ways. Thus, there cannot be a necessary and sufficient condition for preferring a to b, [Putnam's example of a machine's mental state], even if we take "necessary" in the sense of physically necessary . . . .'[6]

Occasionally I detect a whiff of a weaker argument in Putnam, but whether or not it is in Putnam, we should consider this weaker a posteriori argument about the status of (C): even if such premises are not now known to be true, we now have no reason to think that they are false, and it would therefore now be unreasonable to subscribe to a material-mental property identity theory.

As I said, it would be promising for the case of the identity of social and material/mental properties if this argument were sound, or if it were reasonable to believe that it was sound, or if at any rate we had no reason to believe that it was unsound, because we could hope to repeat the argument for the social-material/mental case, and thus block the identification of social properties with material or mental properties. Unfortunately for this possibility, I think we now have some reason to believe that (C) and (D) are false, and hence have reason to believe that the argument is in fact unsound. This shall not encourage us to export to the case of the social such defective merchandise. I do not wish to commit myself on whether mental properties can be identified with material properties. I only claim that the argument from alternative realisations does not succeed in showing that they cannot be so identified.

The Turing Machine evidence does not support a premiss such as (C), in the way in which Putnam must be assuming. From the fact that a Turing Machine can be realised 'in a host of totally different ways' if it can be realised at all, how could it follow that no material property sufficient for preferring a to b can be necessary for the Turing Machine's preferring a to b? Suppose there is some non-disjunctive material property M which is sufficient for a Turing Machine to prefer a to b. What Putnam perhaps shows is that no such non-disjunctive material property, which is sufficient, could also be nomologically necessary, because there are 'a host of totally different' material states similarly nomologically sufficient for the Turing Machine's preferring a to b. But it certainly does not follow that no disjunctive material property (or, that no disjunction of material properties, if these do not yield properties in their own right) is nomologically necessary for preferring a to b. Let's look at this in some more detail. First, some philosophers argue, as I indicated earlier, that the disjunction of two properties, or the negation of a property, may not itself be a property. But I assume that the alternative realisation argument does not accept that mental properties can be identified with disjunctions of material properties, even if these disjunctions do not themselves count as material properties, any more than it accepts identification of mental properties with material properties themselves. No supporter of the alternative realisation argument has ever said, as far as I know, that the argument depends on restricting the idea of a property in such a way that not all disjunctions of properties are themselves properties. Anyway, materialism seems unharmed if the only concession that it is forced to make is that mental properties are identical with disjunctions of material properties, rather than material properties themselves. The qualification is not metaphysically important concerning the question of the nature of the mental.

Second, I assume that if property P is nomologically

sufficient for R and property Q is nomologically sufficient for R, then the disjunctive property, or the disjunction, (P or Q), is nomologically sufficient for R. That is, I assume that if $N(x)(Px \subset Rx)$ and if $N(x)(Qx \subset Rx)$, then $N(x(Px$ or $Qx \subset Rx)$. This inference is valid in any reasonable system of modal logic, and indeed in some unreasonable ones as well.[7] If each of two properties is nomologically sufficient for a third, the disjunction of the two is nomologically sufficient for the third.

Now, *if* there is more to full-blown nomologicity than nomologically necessary and sufficient conditions for something's happening, this assumption may not be valid for nomologicity itself. It may be a law of nature that whatever is P is R, and it may be a law of nature that whatever is Q is R, but yet it may be no law of nature that whatever is P or Q is R (this is controversial). David Armstrong gives, as one of his reasons for denying that all disjunctions of properties are themselves properties, that such a view breaks the link between properties of things and their causal powers.[8] We can construe this as the claim that it may be in virtue of being P that something is R, and it may also be in virtue of being Q that something is R, but false that something is R in virtue of being either P or Q. Again, this is controversial. What is *not* controversial is that it is valid to infer the nomological sufficiency of a disjunction from the nomological sufficiency of each disjunct. Even if full-blown nomologicity were lost under disjunction, nomological sufficiency is not lost under disjunction.

That there are some material properties nomologically sufficient for preferring a to b is conceded by the proponents of the alternative realisation argument. Could there be some set s of all such properties? I cannot think of any reason to deny that there could be. Some of the material properties in set s will have no actual instances, since they will be properties such that, counterfactually, if anything had such a property true of it, it would prefer a to b. There may even be good nomic reasons why nothing actually had some material property, and yet it be true that that property is nomologically sufficient for preferring a to b.

Moreover, not all material properties extensionally sufficient for preferring a to b will be in the set of material properties nomologically sufficient for preferring a to b. For example, suppose that as a matter of coincidence every creature that shows a dimple when smiling prefers a to b. If so, then the property of showing a dimple when smiling would be extensionally sufficient for preferring a to b. But it would not be nomologically sufficient, because it would not support counterfactual subjunctives. In short, the set s includes all those material properties such that, necessarily and not just coincidentally, if anything does have or were to have one of those properties, it prefers or would prefer a to b. Not all extensionally sufficient material properties are also nomologically sufficient for preferring a to b, but the converse does hold. If a material property is nomologically sufficient for preferring a to b, it is extensionally sufficient for it. That this is so is clear in the case of material properties which have instances. In the cases of nomologically suffic-ient material properties with no actual instances, their extensional sufficiency follows simply from the fact that any conditional with a false antecedent is itself true.

Finally, consider the disjunctive material property, or the disjunction (if the disjunction of such properties is not itself a property), which has each of the material properties in set s as a disjunct. If the material properties in set s are $M_1 \ldots M_n$, then the property, or disjunction, that we want to consider is $(M_1$ or M_2 or $\ldots M_n)$. Let's call this disjunctive property or disjunction M^*. What is the relation between M^* and the mental property of preferring a to b? We know that M^* must be nomologically sufficient for preferring a to b, because each of its disjuncts is, so: $N(x(M^*x \subset x$ prefers a to b).

Is M^* nomologically necessary for preferring a to b? M^* must at least be extensionally necessary, since, from the way in which we described set s of properties, it will be clear that, at the very least, nothing which actually prefers a to b will fail to have one of the disjunct material properties from M^* true of it. So, $(x)(x$ prefers a to b $\subset M^*x)$. It seems, then, that the proponent of the alternative realisation argument, in support of premiss (C) or (D), must argue that this extensional necessity of M^* for preferring a to b cannot be strengthened to a nomological necessity, that M^* cannot be nomologically necessary for preferring a to b. For if it can be so strengthened, we will have discovered a material property, or disjunction of material properties, which is nomologically necessary and sufficient for a mental property, the property of preferring a to b. And if we can do this, the alternative realisation argument only shows the simple and uncontroversial truth that as a matter of fact no mental property is identical with a non-disjunctive material property, but only with a complex, disjunctive material property, or with a disjunction of material properties.

If we argue that it cannot be so strengthened, we should be arguing in effect that no matter what properties we add as disjuncts of M^*, we would never arrive at a true subjunctive counterfactual of the form: if any being were to prefer a to b, it would have to have one of those disjunct material properties true of it. But this is not plausible. To begin with, I cannot imagine how one might demonstrate that this is so a priori. This makes me extremely sceptical of those who, unlike Putnam, think that they can show a priori that premisses like (C) and (D) are true. Any argument which purports to show that (C) or (D) is true must, in effect, show why (for example) the extensional truth that whatever prefers a to b has property M^* true of it is not a nomological truth as well, and no allegedly a priori argument I have seen gives the slightest grounds for thinking this.

If we return to the claim that (C) or (D) can be known a posteriori to be true, let us ask whether we have any reason to believe that no disjunctive material property, however complex, or no disjunction of material properties, can be nomologically necessary for some mental property, like the property of preferring a to b. I know of no empirical evidence that would suggest that this is so. I therefore cannot see that we now have any empirical reason for thinking that (C) or (D) is true.

Do we now have any reason for thinking that (C) or (D) is false? I think that we do. Consider what we should have to accept if we believed that there was no true nomologically necessary generalisation that said that whenever some creature preferred a to b, there was a material property, or disjunction of material properties, M^*, that was true of it. We should have to say that regardless of how many disjuncts occurred in M^*, it was a brute, unprojectible fact that that was all the material properties there were such that, if any creature preferred a to b, it had one of those properties true of it. Although this is a matter of empirical speculation, it seems to me that we know enough about the world to expect that the laws of nature will circumscribe in *some* way or other material properties that can be true of any possible creature that prefers a to b. This conjecture can only be known to be true with any degree of certainty from the vantage point of an underlying theory which places restrictions on suitable material structures for mental states, a theory we do not yet possess. But, even in the absence of this theory, we have some empirical reason to expect that there will be *some* restrictions on suitable structures, given what we know about the world in general, and therefore I think we are now able to say that we have *some* reason to think that (C) and (D) are false.

The list of material properties that can be true of an actual or nomologically possible creature which prefers a to b must be very long, perhaps infinite, and it may be quite beyond the capacity of a finite being to enumerate them. But this is not as serious a difficulty as it may seem. The way in which the laws of nature circumscribe the material properties we are looking for (we may speculate) is by selecting a range within which those infinite number of properties must fall. Giving the restrictions on the range of properties, each of which is nomologically sufficient for a specific mental property, is in effect to give a formula for generating that infinite number of properties, the having of some one of which is nomologically necessary for that specific mental property. The idea would be that only material properties within a certain specifiable range are suitable for realising some mental property, and there may be an infinite number of such material properties within that specifiable range.

As I admitted, without the theory, all of this is conjectural. But I cannot see that we have any empirical evidence to suggest that it is false, and I think that our empirical beliefs about the general nature of the world suggest that these conjectures are true. If it is in virtue of a law of nature that *only* n material properties are nomologically sufficient for realising some mental state, where 'n' might be an infinite number of properties within a certain range, then having some one of those n material properties is nomologically necessary for being in that mental state. And that is an end to the matter. 'Any creature who prefers a to b has one of those n number of material properties true of it' will support counterfactuals and have nomic force. There will, indeed, be a material property, or disjunction of material properties, nomologically necessary and sufficient for mental properties like preferring a to b.

Putnam is not, to be sure, unaware of the possibility of the sort of reply that I have made to the alternative possible realisation argument. In his paper, 'Philosophy and our mental life', Putnam considers the suggestion that one may be able to 'define a psychological state as a disjunction, the individual disjuncts being . . . conjunctions of a machine state and a tape (i.e. a total description of the content of the memory bank)'.[9] Putnam then dismisses this reply in seven brief lines. His objections seem two-fold.

First, 'such a description would be literally infinite.' We have already seen some reason for thinking that such a description might be given in terms of a finite list of material properties (machine states), which provide the limits between which the infinite number of appropriate material properties (machine states) must fall. Moreover, two questions must be carefully distinguished: (a) what is the metaphysical truth about mental properties, and (b) what will a fully developed psychological theory look like, what form will it take? Putnam is primarily addressing (b); I am interested in (a). An infinity of material properties (or machine states), if there is one, all of which might be the realisation of some mental or psychological property, will bear on the two questions quite differently. If there were an infinity of such material properties or machine states, suppose that this did spell doom for the attempt to cast a psychological theory in a machine-state form. But it may be quite irrelevant to the answer to the metaphysical question.

Compare this to the attempted reductive identification of physical objects with sets of actual and possible sensory experiences. This reductive identification, although it has many other difficulties which perhaps it cannot meet, does *not* founder, from a metaphysical point of view, on the infinity of such actual and possible sensory experiences. On the other hand, the infinity of such actual and possible sensory experiences might preclude casting a *theory* of physical objects in a sensory-experience form.

Putnam's second objection cannot be pursued here. He says that 'the machine table description . . . is as removed from the description *via* a psychological theory as the physico-chemical description is'. This second objection rests on a suggestive but barely developed account of explanation, which leans heavily on the idea that, in an explanation, the explanans must refer to 'structurally relevant' features of the situation. Putnam supposes, then, that the machine states and tapes are, like physical and chemical states, not structurally relevant in an explanation or account of the psychological.

Putnam does not offer any characterisation of the idea of explanatory relevance that he requires. I turn to the topic of explanation in chapter 4. More to the point here, this second objection again addresses (b) rather than (a). I conclude that Putnam offers no good reason for dismissing the empirical speculation according to which mental properties can be reductively identified with disjunctive material properties or disjunctions of material properties.

Social properties and alternative realisations

The argument from alternative realisations fails to provide us with a sound argument on its home territory, the philosophy of mind, which lessens the attractions of its potential export for arguing for the irreducibility of the social to the material/mental. Indeed, we might wonder whether we could not export its failure as a sound argument in the context of the philosophy of mind, in order to predict its unsoundness if used to block the reduction of social to material/mental properties. Could we not empirically speculate, as we did before, that there will be material/mental properties (or disjunctions thereof) nomologically necessary and sufficient for social properties, and hence (on the proposed identity criterion) with which they are identical?

I think that this sort of speculation is far less compelling in the case of social properties than it was in the case of the philosophy of mind. I intend my remarks in this section merely to caution against an immediate conclusion that the alternative realisation argument, if unsound in the philosophy of mind, will be equally unsound in the philosophy of social science. That is, my remarks will, I hope, suggest why the empirical speculation that might incline one in favour of the supposition that there are material properties, or disjunctions thereof, nomologically necessary and sufficient for mental properties, has greater intuitive appeal than does the empirical speculation needed to support the thought that there are material/mental properties, or disjunctions thereof, which are nomologically necessary and sufficient for social properties. I return, at the end of the chapter, to further remarks which I hope will be more than merely suggestive. I do in fact believe that the use of the alternative realisation argument in the philosophy of social science, concerning the alleged reduction of social to material/mental properties, is sound.

In the case of the alleged reduction of mental to material properties, speculation concerning the unsoundness of the alternative realisation argument, which attempts to block the reduction, was based on the thought that there were lawlike restrictions on the material properties nomologically sufficient for mental properties. The analogous thought seems less convincing in the case of social properties. Of course, there are bound to be material or mental properties, or negations of such properties (if these are not themselves properties) which are nomologically necessary for social properties – e.g. perhaps nothing made only of liquid iodine and californium could be a mayor. No one would suggest that there were no material or mental restrictions of any kind on the social. But the question at isssue is this: are there nomic restrictions concerning which material and mental properties can be sufficient for some social property, so that the disjunction of these nomologically sufficient material/mental properties is itself nomologically necessary for the social property? Is there some set of material/mental properties, each nomologically sufficient for being a mayor, such that, if someone were to be a mayor, he would have to have some property from that set true of him?

I would not speculate that the answer to these questions was in the affirmative, as I did in the case of the material and the mental. My reason is this. One might believe that *which* properties were nomologically sufficient for being a mayor was, in part, something conventional, something not wholly dictated to us by the material or mental structure of reality. Human beings have a part in choosing what the material and mental world has to be like, such that being that way makes it true that someone is a mayor. It isn't just in virtue of the laws of nature that certain arrangements of mind and matter are sufficient for the realisation of social properties. It's also in virtue of how we decide to construct the social world.

At this point in the chapter, I do not ask the reader to accept these thoughts as true, but only as making the empirical speculation in favour of the unsoundness of the alternative realisation argument that I advanced in the previous section as less immediately compelling in the case now before us, the case of social properties. As I said, I will return to this more fully at the end of the chapter, where I try to make more credible the thought that whatever its faults in the philosophy of mind, the argument from alternative realisations is a great deal more plausible in blocking the reduction of social to material/mental properties.

What are social properties?

I want to begin by considering a quite distinct line of argument for the question of the reducibility of social properties. First, though, I want to be clearer about what makes a property a *social* property. It will not do to try to characterise a property as social in virtue of the type of entity having that property, since material, mental, and social entities can all have social properties. Even if a person were a special sort of embodied mental entity, he could be a mayor. A piece of plastic, a material thing, can be a credit card. A nation, a social entity, can join a confederation. Yet the properties asserted of these three different kinds of things are all social properties. That a property is social has something to do with the property itself, rather than that to which it applies.

There is a tendency, especially in the literature critical of individualism, to locate this special feature of social properties in their relationality. In a recent book, Alan Garfinkel argues for the irreducibility of social explanations to individualistic ones. In the following quotation, he uses 'atomistically' to mean 'unrelated' and 'structural relations' to mean 'irreducible social relations' (or 'macro-level', as he calls them): 'The essence of this critique of the market lies in insisting on the structural relations that hold among individuals. The classical conception of the market sees individuals atomistically. . . .'[10] Garfinkel begins with the perfectly sound point that one cannot understand human economic activity apart from the relations that exist between the economic agents. However, Garfinkel, without further argument, refers to such relations as 'structural', by which he intends that the relations are irreducibly social. He overlooks the possibility that all the relations that exist between persons are non-social, or are reducible to non-social, relations. Since there certainly are at least some non-social relations between persons, we still need to know in virtue of what a property is social, if not simply in virtue of its relationality.

Let's start by contrasting two relational properties, the first intuitively non-social and the second intuitively social: the property of jointly bearing the weight of a stone, and the property of paying for a stone. The property of jointly bearing the weight of a stone might be true of two or more inanimate objects, but it also might be true of two or more persons. Still, even when true of persons, it does not ascribe a social relation to them. The two individuals might jointly bear the weight of a stone as a matter of fact of which they were completely unaware, and of which anyone else was unaware. What is the difference between these two relational properties which accounts for the fact that only one of them is a social relational property?

Unlike what might be the case when x and y jointly bear the weight of a stone, if x pays y for a stone, there is a characteristic system of interlocking beliefs and expectations whose existence is entailed by the social property's applicability. It would not damage my argument if I were forced to concede the possibility of non-standard, odd cases in which the specific individuals related by the social relation fail to have any of these beliefs and expectations, so that I might unintentionally pay you for a stone while we were briefly visiting Borneo, both of us being completely unaware that what we were doing counted, in Borneo, as paying someone for a stone. In such a case, there is still a nested system of beliefs involved, though the beliefs are not located in the standard place, viz. the participants to the transaction. The characteristic system of interlocking beliefs and expectations will exist, because our Borneian observers will certainly have them. In claiming that the applicability of a social relation between x and y entails the existence of an interlocking system of beliefs and expectations, it does not necessarily follow that in all cases x and y must share those beliefs and expectations, although I think that the cases in which they fail to share them are necessarily parasitic on the standard cases in which they do (nothing in my argument depends on my belief that these non-standard cases are parasitic on the standard ones). In what follows, I consider only the standard case in which the agents related by the social relation share in the system of beliefs and expectations, but all of what follows must be understood so as to permit the possibility of non-standard cases, if indeed they are possible.

A rather different sort of problem is this. To use an example that I will be employing in a moment, normally paying someone for something involves expectations that he will surrender it in exchange for what I am to give him and that he will not try to regain it without my consent. On a specific occasion, I may be paying Al Capone for something, knowing full well that he will refuse to deliver the goods as expected, or, if he does deliver, that he will creep back when I am unaware and repossess what I bought from him. Let's even suppose that Capone is himself aware that I fail to have the normal expectations about what he will do. Indeed, suppose no one in the whole society expects Capone to surrender what he is meant to surrender, or not to retake what he surrenders if he does so. I do not know if this would still be a case of my paying Capone for something in our legal system, because failure of intent might be important in determining whether I have paid him for something. But whether or not it is true in our legal system that, in such a case, I have paid Capone for something, there is no difficulty in supposing a legal system (perhaps ours is like this) in which intention plays no part in the definition of some act like a sale. If this is so, then if Capone and I go through certain recognised acts, then I have paid him for something, in spite of the complete breakdown in the normal expectations and beliefs about purchase and sale in the particular case.

But this leaves my claim undisturbed. If I pay Capone for a stone, it follows that there is a system of beliefs and expectations of the kind I shall describe, even if those beliefs and expectations do not attach to our specific acts on this particular occasion. And this is surely correct. It is essential to the case of purchasing something from Capone that there is this general system of beliefs and expectations that attach to purchase and sale; if this were not so, whatever we were doing could not be a *paying* by me, to Capone, for something. In what follows, for ease of exposition, the examples I discuss are ones in which the beliefs and expectations attach not only generally to acts of that kind, but to the specific acts of the agents of whom the social relation is true. Again, nothing depends on this, and all of what follows must be understood to permit the possibility of these non-standard cases.

Nested systems: the first and second components

What is such a system of interlocking beliefs and expectations like? I will claim that a necessary and sufficient condition for a relational property P being a social relational property is that, if x and y stand in the relation P, then it follows that a nested system of interlocking beliefs and expectations exists. I use 'nested system' in a technical sense. Thus, to assess my contention, it is essential to be precise about in what such a nested system consists. I shall argue that there are four parts or components of a nested system that can be distinguished, each part being necessary and the four being jointly sufficient for the existence of a nested system. It is only when the existence of a nested system in this technical sense follows from a relational property P's being true of at least two things (persons, objects, or whatever) that P is a social relational property.

I begin, then, by singling out only two of the four conditions for the existence of a nested system. My strategy is to uncover the final two by seeing why it is that the presence of these two parts alone is insufficient for the obtaining of any social relation. The first condition for the existence of a nested system is this: if there are any social relations between x and y, x and y will have interlocking beliefs and expectations about actions (where this category must be taken sufficiently widely so as to permit mental actions). In the case of x paying y for a stone, x will expect y to surrender the stone in return for something that x gives y, and x will expect that y will not try and regain control of the stone unless in return for something x willingly accepts from y. Matching and interlocking beliefs and expectations are held by y about x. Y will expect x to give him something in return for the stone and y will not expect to regain control of the stone with x's consent unless in return for something x willingly accepts from him.

But these beliefs and expectations are insufficient. The second condition for the existence of the required system of beliefs and expectations are interlocking beliefs and expectations about beliefs and expectations (or second-order beliefs and expectations). In the standard case, x believes that y has these beliefs and expectations; y believes that x has these beliefs and expectations; x believes that y believes that x has them; y believes that x believes that y has them; and so on. The 'and so on' is not intended to generate a vicious regress. The regress is limited by the natural ability of agents to form third- or fourth-order beliefs and expectations, so wherever the reader believes these limits fall, there he may think of the regress as brought to an end. The beliefs in question will typically only be dispositional rather than occurrent.

Even though these first two components, beliefs and expectations about actions and beliefs and expectations about beliefs and expectations, are insufficient for composing a nested system of beliefs and expectations in the technical sense I need that will help us get at the idea of a social relation, they are certainly sufficient for distinguishing between jointly bearing the weight of a stone and paying for a stone and sufficient for seeing why the former is not a social relation. When x and y jointly bear the weight of a stone, such beliefs and expectations may or may not exist, so their existence does not follow from the ascription of the relational property, jointly bearing the weight of a stone. But their existence does follow in the case of the application of the social relational property, purchasing a stone from. Still, although these first two components of a nested system are sufficient for distinguishing between the non-social relational property, jointly bearing the weight of a stone, and the social relational property, purchasing a stone, they are insufficient for distinguishing between all cases of non-social and social relational properties, as we shall soon see.

Nested systems: the third and fourth components

Anthony Quinton says that: 'What is characteristic of the relations studied by the social sciences is that they involve consciousness of each other by the people related'.[11] Quinton's claim is on the right lines, but too weak. In thinking about why Quinton's claim is too weak, we shall see why the first two components of a nested system – beliefs and expectations about actions, second-order

110

(perhaps even higher-order) beliefs and expectations about beliefs and expectations – are insufficient for the existence of a nested system, in the sufficiently full technical sense to permit that latter idea to distinguish between all social and non-social relational properties.

The insufficiency of Quinton's proposed criterion for 'what is characteristic of the social sciences' can be brought out by means of the following example. Suppose that there were two tribes, A and B, on either side of a mountain, both tribes having strong taboos which prevent them from crossing the mountain. The two tribes thus lack any awareness of each other's existence. We introduce young Marco Polo into our story. On his travels, he first visits tribe A. He then crosses the mountain and discovers tribe B. He tells tribe B about tribe A and tells B that he will tell A about B's existence on his return trip. This he does, and neither tribe has any contact with, or learns anything further about, the other after Marco Polo's departure. Intuitively, there are no social relations between the two tribes, in spite of the fact that they are fully aware of each other's existence. So consciousness of one another may be necessary, but it is not sufficient, for the existence of social relations (perhaps Quinton did not intend to be giving a sufficient condition in saying what he thought was 'characteristic' of the relations studied by the social sciences).

We can use this same story to show why the first two components of a nested system that I have so far mentioned are insufficient, if we are to use nested systems to distinguish between social and non-social relations. Consider the relation that holds between the two tribes, A and B. A has beliefs about the existence of B, and B believes that A has these beliefs. B has beliefs about the existence of A, and A believes that B has these beliefs. But of course the first-order beliefs are not about actions, which was a requirement of our account.

It would not be difficult to amend our story so that this requirement was met. Suppose Marco Polo leaves each tribe with a very powerful and tall periscope-like instrument, so that they can minutely observe each other's behaviour and activity. Being curious, they begin to amass a great deal of information about one another's doings. They develop an intimate knowledge of each other's social life. Moreover, suppose Marco Polo has told both tribes that the other would have an instrument identical to theirs, and has told each tribe that the other was capable of perfecting a knowledge as complete as it itself could. If we presume all this, it may well happen that all the beliefs and expectations we have discussed as forming part of a nested set might develop. They will be conscious not only of one another's existence, but each will be conscious of the activities of the other. Moreover, the second-order beliefs and expectations may occur. Tribe A believes that tribe B will do certain things, and tribe B believes that tribe A has these beliefs about it. Tribe B believes that tribe A will do certain things, and tribe A believes that tribe B has these beliefs about it. We can imagine this developing to whatever degree of nestedness we care to hypothesise, and still, I think, it will be admitted that something essential for there being a social relation has been omitted. What more is needed?

In the story so far, there are certainly relations between actions on the one hand and beliefs and expectations on the other. What tribe B does can be a reason for what tribe A believes, because tribe A believes that tribe B is doing something partly because B is doing that thing. The beliefs of tribe A (e.g. the belief that B is doing something) can themselves *be* reasons as well as be *held* for reasons, because tribe B believes that tribe A believes that B is doing something, in part because tribe A does believe that B is doing something. One of the reasons for tribe B's believing that tribe A believes that B is doing something is tribe A's belief that B is doing that thing. Note that these beliefs and expectations are ascending, in this sense: an action can be a reason for a belief or expectation about an action, and a belief or expectation of order n can be a reason for a belief or expectation of order $n + 1$. But no belief or expectation of order n is a reason for a belief or expectation of order $n - 1$, nor is a belief or expectation about an action a reason for acting in some way.

No one likes to be the subject of scientific observation unwillingly. Suppose tribe A, believing that B believes that it will do something, decides to do something else as a way of falsifying B's belief. Both tribes might start altering their activities as a strategy for defeating the expectations of the other. That is, the role of the beliefs and expectations alter, so that they begin to play what I refer to as a descending role; one of the reasons for A's altering its behaviour is A's belief about what B expects that A will do. Social actors react not only to what each other do, because physical objects can do this, but they also react to what they believe others believe that they will do. Let's require, then, for the existence of a nested set of beliefs and expectations, not only the two conditions already mentioned (beliefs and expectations about action; higher-order beliefs and expectations about beliefs and expectations), but *also* a third condition, namely that some descending reason-relations exist among them. Descending reason-relations exist among such beliefs, expectations, and actions if some belief or expectation about how others believe or expect an agent to act is at least part of that agent's reason for acting in some way. An analogous requirement to that of descending reason-relations is built in by Shwayder to his analysis of community rules by the condition that one acts in some way because he *believes* that others believe that he will act from the belief that they expect him to act in some way.[12] The similarity between our accounts resides in the fact that he too requires that one's actions are sometimes partly motivated by beliefs about what others expect or believe.

Of course, I am not saying that social relations exist only when social actors alter their behaviour in order to outwit one another by falsifying beliefs about what they will do. More often than not, I do something partly because it is what I believe that others believe or expect that I will do. Social co-operation assumes that this happens. So what is crucial for the existence of social relations between people is that they sometimes do what they do (and this includes altering what they are doing to defeat those expectations as a special case), whether to achieve co-operation or deception, partly as a consequence of the beliefs they have about the beliefs or expectations others have about what they will do. If we add this third requirement, that of descending reason-relations, to what is needed for a system of nested beliefs to exist, is the fact that the existence of a nested system (with only these three components) follows from the obtaining of a relation P necessary and sufficient for P's being a social relation?

There is, I fear, a final complication. Suppose tribe A alters what it does because of its beliefs about what tribe B expects it to do, and suppose tribe B alters what it does because of its beliefs about what tribe A expects it to do. But suppose tribe B is not aware that tribe A is altering its behaviour for these reasons, and similarly that tribe A is not aware that tribe B is altering its behaviour for these reasons. If so, they may simply think of their expectations and beliefs about the behaviour of the other as falsified because based on insufficient or faulty empirical data about the other's activities. The fourth condition which is necessary in order for there to be social relations between them is that A believes that B sometimes does what it does for these reasons (i.e. A believes that sometimes B does what it does because of its, B's, belief about what A believes that B will do), and that B believes that A sometimes does what it does for these reasons (i.e. B believes that sometimes A does what it does because of its, A's, belief about what B believes that A will do). Note that this fourth requirement is again one of an 'ascending' relation. In social life, agents respond to the beliefs and expectations of others (the third requirement), and this is generally believed to be the case (the fourth requirement).

To sum up, then, a relation P is a social relation iff it follows from the fact that P obtains that a system of nested beliefs and expectations exists. A nested system of beliefs and expectations exists iff (1) there is an interlocking set of beliefs and expectations about the actions of agents, (2) there is an interlocking set of higher-order beliefs and expectations about beliefs and expectations, (3) there are some descending reason-relations among these beliefs, expectations and actions, so that sometimes what agents do is a consequence of their beliefs or expectations about what other agents believe or expect that they will do, and (4) it is generally believed that (3) is true. When conditions (1)-(4) obtain, it

114

seems to me intuitive that a point has been reached at which we are willing to concede that specifically *social* relations obtain between the agents mentioned in the four conditions.

I should like to add several points by way of explanation or clarification. First, as I mentioned before, 'activity' and 'behaviour' should be understood widely, so as to include mental acts. In the descending reason-chains the ultimate stopping places need not be physical actions. There could be social relations between mathematicians who had nested beliefs about the proofs each other were working on in their heads, and who sometimes changed their mental activity in the light of the beliefs they held about what others believed about their mental activity. Even more dramatically, I cannot see why there could not be social relations between disembodied minds (if it is logically possible that there be disembodied minds), as long as such beings could form the requisite nested beliefs and expectations about one another's mental activity with the requisite direction of reasons between them. It seems to be a point in favour of my analysis that it does not make impossible the idea of social relations between disembodied minds.

Second, it is no requirement of my analysis that P itself turn up in the description of the behaviour or activity which the nested beliefs or expectations are ultimately about. For example, the social relation between x and y might be one of economic exploitation, and both x and y, and indeed even social agents generally, might be quite unaware of this exploitation and what it means to their lives. Social actors, even whole communities, do not always understand their social life, which may remain opaque to them. They may be victims of false consciousness, as it is sometimes called. Yet, it may still be true that social relations of exploitation exist among members of that community. If so, from the fact that x exploits y, it follows that there is *some* set of nested beliefs and expectations in the sense that I have explained, but the beliefs and expectations in the required set might not be *about* exploitation, because the concept of exploitation may not be available to x or y or to anyone else in the community. The beliefs and expectations which are necessary for the social relation of exploitation holding between

115

any two agents may be beliefs and expectations about the rights and duties of the employer and the employee, or other beliefs that embody commonsense ideas that are available to the social agents.

Third, the analysis of a property's being a social property that I have offered shows why all social properties are relational. The reason is this: if any social property is true of anything, it follows that an appropriately nested system of interlocking beliefs and expectations exists. But a nested system of these beliefs and expectations can only exist if at least two persons exist. Therefore, if any social property is true of anything, at least two persons exist; no social property can be true of anything in a universe in which there is only one person and *a fortiori* no social property can be true of anything in a universe in which there is only one object. All social properties are therefore relational properties, by the test of relationality that I offered in chapter 1.

Fourth, I have spoken in terms of the existence of the nested system following from the obtaining of the relational property, not from its mere existence. This is to *allow* for the possibility that uninstantiated social properties exist (I expect intuitions to differ about this, perhaps even more so than intuitions about the existence of uninstantiated properties generally). Margaret Mead might wrongly identify some social institution in a primitive society as one of engaging in kitchiboo. It may be that, in fact, no person anywhere has ever engaged in this practice that she wrongly locates in this primitive society. If so, it may be that the social property of engaging in kitchiboo exists (M.M. might have given us a very precise account of what is involved in this property of engaging in kitchiboo, in spite of the fact that it has never been true of anyone), and yet no appropriate system of nested beliefs has ever existed anywhere. On our criterion, we can still see why engaging in kitchiboo counts as a social property: if it were to hold of some individual, then it would follow that a nested system of beliefs existed.

Fifth, the account of social properties that I offer here is similar in some respects to one given by David Shwayder, in *The Stratification of Behaviour*,[13] with one difference of special importance. His account is not of a social property, but of a social rule: 'Community rules are systems of expectations'; 'The rule is, as it were, a system of community, mutual expectations' (pp. 252-3). I think that an account in terms of nested systems, although strong enough to capture the idea of a social property, is not strong enough to capture the idea of a social rule.[14] Consider for example a situation in which a customary practice has grown up between people of a certain society to drink tea at breakfast. There may well be a nested system of interlocking beliefs and expectations between them about these tea drinkings, and it certainly does seem right to say that there is a social relation between them, for they share a practice or custom to do this. But what they may not share is a rule to do so, as H.L.A. Hart reminds us in *The Concept of Law* by distinguishing between rules and (mere) convergent behaviour. The idea of a rule is a stronger idea; in my view it includes the idea of 'pressures for conformity', for one has rules about what one must do willy-nilly. And they may not regard their practice or custom of tea drinking in this light. Since social relations so commonly take a coercive form, it is easy to confuse the idea of the social generally with the more specific idea of a social rule. These are, though, quite distinct ideas, and I offer an account, similar in content to Shwayder's but of the idea of a social property rather than that of a social rule.

Finally, social relations can hold between persons and persons (e.g. being the godfather of), between persons and objects (e.g. renting), and objects and objects (e.g. costing more than). In my account, I considered cases in which the social relations relate persons and persons. This is the simplest case, and the analysis can easily be extended for the other cases. Nothing in my analysis depends on restricting the applicability of social relations to persons in any way; on the other hand, I confess to the Marxian belief that cases of social relations obtaining between persons and objects or between objects and objects are entirely parasitic on the cases in which they obtain between persons and persons. The denial of this belief is what Marx calls 'fetishism'.[15]

The irreducibility of social to mental properties

Now that we have some grasp of what makes a property a social property, it will be easier, I think, to return to our main question concerning the reducibility of social to mental properties. My claim is: a property P is a social property iff from the fact that P applies to anything, it follows that a nested system of beliefs and expectations exists. It might seem an easy step to conclude from this that social properties were themselves mental properties, or sets thereof. Can social property P be reductively identified with the set of mental properties which go into making up the nested system in question (plus perhaps the requisite ascending and descending reason-relation between them)? Specific analyses of social properties in terms of parts of the nest would be suggested. Would such analyses be reductive? For example, can the social property of paying y for a stone just *be* the mental properties of expecting y to surrender the stone in return for something given to y, expecting y will not try to regain control of the stone unless in return for something willingly accepted from y, and so on? It might seem that, from the description of the beliefs and expectations in the nested system, one should be able to extract sufficient mental properties, like the properties of believing or expecting certain things, with which to reductively identify social properties.

There are two sorts of reasons that I should like to discuss for thinking that this apparently natural development of my analysis of what it is for a property to be a social property is not acceptable. That is, these are reasons for thinking that the analyses of social properties in terms of mental properties are either unavailable or, if available, not reductive. I would not wish to overstate the degree of conclusiveness I take my reasons, or argument sketches, to possess. I do not think that I can demonstrate the unavailability of reductive analyses in terms of mental properties for social properties generally. Rather, I select certain important subsets of social properties. Even for the subsets, my anti-reductive arguments are not conclusive. The first argument appeals to a certain amount of empirical hypothesis. Indeed,

118

in the first argument, I briefly return to the question of alternative realisations. I did not take that argument to be successful in the philosophy of mind. I offered some considerations for not extrapolating its *lack* of success in the philosophy of mind to the philosophy of social science. I will mention some further considerations about social properties which suggest that the alternative realisation argument might indeed be successful after all in blocking the reduction of social to mental properties.

I think that my second argument is far more powerful than the first. Still, the reader will see that even my second argument rests on a premiss which I regard as overwhelmingly likely, but for which I advance no independent argument.

The first anti-reductive argument

I have argued that a property P is a social property iff it follows from the fact that P is true of something that there is *some* nested system of beliefs and expectations. One can distinguish two sorts of social properties: variable and non-variable. A social property is non-variable iff there is some specific system of beliefs and expectations that must exist whenever the property is true of something. For example, consider the social property, engaging in the (British) custom of drinking tea at breakfast. If this property is true of a person, it follows that there is a *specific* system of beliefs and expectations that must exist, for in general we will expect one another to drink tea at breakfast. Since this is so, I call the social property of participating in the custom of drinking tea at breakfast 'a non-variable social property'.

Most social properties are not like this; most social properties are variable. If a variable social property obtains, it follows that some nested system or other must exist, but there is no nested system whose existence is entailed by the obtaining of the variable social property. Suppose P is a variable social property. Then, if P is true of x, nested system s_1 might exist. If P is true of y (who may live in another society at a different time than x) nested system s_2

might exist. The applicability of these social properties requires only that *a* nested system exists, but that requirement might be filled at one time by one system and at another time by another.

As an example of a variable social property, consider the property of being a mayor. What nested system of beliefs and expectations must exist when it is true of some person that he is a mayor? What he or other people believe or expect of one another when a person is a mayor will depend on the duties and responsibilities of his office. These depend on social convention, and can vary indefinitely. When someone is a mayor, there must be some nested system of beliefs and expectations widely shared. But there are few, if any, restrictions, on the sorts of things a society could expect a mayor to do. Therefore, there are few, if any, restrictions on the range of nested systems that might exist when someone is a mayor. It might be expected of a mayor to do almost anything.

I professed myself less than happy with the use of the alternative realisation argument in the philosophy of mind. The idea there was that, even if there are many alternative possible realisations for a mental property, it appeared plausible to think that there were some natural restrictions on the range of suitable properties, and, if so, mental properties could after all be reductively identified with complex, disjunctive material properties (or disjunctions of material properties). I speculated that there would not be the same nomological restrictions of a significant kind on the range of material or mental properties suitable for realising social properties. My account of social properties in terms of nested systems of believings and expectings, in conjunction with the distinction between non-variable and variable social properties, reinforces the strength of the speculation that the alternative realisation argument might after all be sound when used in the philosophy of social science. Given the unrestricted things one might expect or believe of a person or object of which a variable social property is true, it seems unlikely that significant range restrictions on the mental properties sufficient for such social properties will be available. If such range restrictions are unavailable, there will not be material/mental properties, or disjunctions thereof, both nomologically necessary and sufficient for a variable social property.

I would say that this first anti-reductivist argument suggests the irreducibility of at least one important kind of social property, but that it is far from decisive. It owes far too much to speculation and intuition. It invites the reader to think of plausible restrictions on the range of mental believings and expectings sufficient for some variable social property like being a mayor, and assumes that the invitation cannot be met. It would be preferable to have an argument that convinces those not already convinced.

The second anti-reductivist argument

The second argument does not attempt to show, like the first, that no analyses of the social in terms of the mental are available. The second argument tries to show that, even if available, analyses of the social in terms of the mental would not be reductive. Such analyses would, I claim, be circular, at least in the case of one important kind of social property. I argue that, for one sort of social property, indeed the most characteristic sort, mental properties adequate for their identification (if any) would themselves presuppose the existence of other social properties. Any such identification would be circular, in the sense in which I explained this idea in chapter 1, and hence non-reductive. However, even this second argument, though stronger than the first, rests on an unargued premiss, which I state but for which I offer no independent argument.

We can again distinguish between two kinds of social properties, weakly social and strongly social properties. I do not wish to commit myself on how this distinction fits with the earlier distinction between non-variable and variable social properties. However, as my example of a weakly social property, I would like to consider the same social property that I used as an example of a non-variable social property: participating in the custom of drinking tea at breakfast. This is a social property, even though the property of drinking tea at breakfast is not a social property. Of course, we might say of someone that he drinks tea at breakfast, its being understood from the context that we mean that he participates in the custom of doing this. But simply to say of someone that he drinks tea at breakfast, even when there is a social custom to do this and when he does it because it is a custom, is not to *say* that some social property is true of the person. On the other hand, the property of participating in the custom of drinking tea at breakfast is a social property, because if it is true of someone, it follows that a nested system of interlocking beliefs and expectations exists. As I have already claimed, the property is a non-variable social property, because a nested system of interlocking beliefs and expectations about tea drinking at breakfast *is* necessary for the property's applicability.

These beliefs and expectations have propositional objects. What are they? They are or include: that some token action of the type, tea drinking at breakfast, will be performed. The beliefs and expectations in the nested systems are characteristically about specific action types, not specific action tokens. What is believed or expected is that some action token or other of a specific type will be done. Although I have said that it is logically possible for there to be social relations between disembodied persons (if it is logically possible for there to be disembodied persons), in fact social relations hold between embodied persons like ourselves. Even so, the propositional objects of the beliefs and expectations which go to make up the nested system can sometimes be: that some mental action token of some specific mental action type will be done. For example, as I suggested earlier, there may be a club of mathematicians which has as one of its rules that between meetings each member will think about some especially important proof. But this kind of example would be atypical. Characteristically, the beliefs and expectations are about non-mental actions. In the case of tea drinking at breakfast, the object of belief or expectation is: that some token of the action type, tea drinking at breakfast, will be performed. Note that the action type (or property) which the belief is about is non-social, in the sense I have already indicated.[16] So, in the example of participating in the custom of drinking tea at breakfast, the associated beliefs and expectations are about non-social action types. I call a social property 'weakly social' when *all* of the beliefs or expectations in the associated nested system have propositional objects of the form, 'Someone will F', where 'F' specifies a non-social action type.

A social property is strongly social when some of the associated beliefs and expectations have propositional objects involving a *social* action type. Consider, again, the social property of being a mayor. I have already argued that this is a variable social property, so it makes no sense to ask that one consider all of the beliefs and expectations that may be associated with any instance of the property. But consider some plausible examples. I expect him to attend certain civic functions. I expect him to sign executive orders. I expect him to offer the keys of the City to selected visiting dignitaries. And so on. That is, what I believe or expect him to do is to perform some action token of a specific *social* action type. Some propositional objects of my beliefs and expectations will have the form: 'Someone will G', where 'G' specifies a social action type. Action types are a special sort of property, and social action types are a special sort of social property.

Reference to social action types will rearise in unpacking the idea of strongly social properties. I may expect the mayor to sign an executive order, and yet have no beliefs or expectations about the physical actions he will undertake in order to sign the order. I may expect him to sign the order, and he may do so by etching his name with a laser beam, but I may not expect him to have done this. Even in those instances in which I do also have beliefs and expectations about his physical actions (perhaps I do expect him to etch his name with a laser), this is insufficient for believing that he will sign an executive order, since someone completely ignorant of the society may form the first belief or expectation while failing to have the second.

The property of believing or expecting that some token of a social action type will be done is a psychological property (or, mental property). Belief and expectation contexts are non-extensional, in the sense that in general there is no inference from 'A believes that x is P' to 'There is an x such that A believes that it is P'. From the fact that I have expectations that the mayor will sign an executive order, it does not follow that there are any executive orders, or even that there are any mayors. I might be as misled as the Margaret Mead of my earlier story, with her theory of kitchiboo. Thus, by my criterion, although the property of signing an executive order is a social property, believing that someone will perform some token action of the social action type, a signing of an executive order, is not a social property (it is a mental property), since the existence of a nested system of beliefs and expectations is not entailed by its correct application.

However, although beliefs and expectations are non-extensional with regard to objects or token acts or events, they are not non-extensional with regard to properties or action types. If I have an intelligible belief that x is P, it does not follow that there is an x, but it does follow that there is a property P such that I believe that x has it. This is, of course, compatible with believing that properties are only sets, or concepts, or anything else one might like. Whatever properties are, if there is an intelligible belief that x is P, there must be the property of being P.[17]

In general, then, believing that someone will perform a token action of the social action type S is a mental and not a social property, but if there is this mental property, it follows that there is some social action type S, or some social property, i.e. engaging in an S-type act. These last *are* social properties on the criterion I have given: *if* instantiated, it follows that some nested system of beliefs and expectations exists. The mental believings and expectings that form the nested systems associated with strongly social properties themselves presuppose, in turn, the existence of social properties (but do not of course presuppose that the social properties are instantiated).

My second argument has, so far, merely unpacked what is involved in the definition of a strongly social property, namely, that a strongly social property is a property such that in its analysis in terms of beliefs and expectations, a further social property will reappear in the analysans. Can we conclude that such analyses, even if available, will be circular? This will not yet follow. Weakly social properties can (by definition) be given social-property-free analyses. Suppose, then, that the first phase of the reduction is from strongly social properties to beliefs and expectations about the instantiation of (only) weakly social properties or weakly social action types. Then there may be a further, second reduction that analyses the weakly social properties or weakly social action types in terms of beliefs and expectations about the instantiation of (only) non-social properties or non-social action types. We cannot hope to have convincingly argued for the irreducibility of strongly social properties unless we can block this possibility.

In order to block this move, I need something stronger than merely the definition of a strongly social property:

(A)   In the analysis of any strongly social property in terms of beliefs and expectations, a further social property will reappear in the analysans.

I need the stronger claim:

(B)   There are at least some strongly social properties such that no analysis of them, however remote, in terms of beliefs and expectations about the instantiation of only weakly social properties and non-social properties can be adequate.[18]

I think that (B) is true. I do not assert that there could not be a recognisably human social life unless there were social properties of the kind mentioned in (B). On the contrary, one can imagine a social life such that only weakly social properties were instantiated, or only strongly social properties which had no further strongly social properties in their analysans. All such social properties could finally be 'reduced' to beliefs and expectations about the instantiation of non-social properties or action types. Such a social life would allow for the ascription of such social properties as: participating in the custom of G-ing, following a public rule to do G, co-operating in G-ing, playing a game that involves doing G (where 'G' specifies a non-social action type).

125

One could conceive of such a social life, and social life may take this form in very primitive and rudimentary societies. But our social life is not like that, for our social life allows for the ascription of strongly social properties concerning which (B) is true. Indeed, it is these social properties that strike us as *most characteristic* of what social life is like. My examples in the discussion of strongly social properties were of this kind. Consider again the strongly social property of being a mayor. What I expect of the mayor is for him to attend certain state functions, sign executive orders, and so on. The instantiations which I expect are *of* further social action types *themselves strongly social*. I could not set out the beliefs and expectations I have when someone attends a state function or signs an executive order without employing further (strongly) social properties or action types. (B), I hold, is true of the social properties that we ascribe and which we take to be most characteristic of what sociality is like.

Since (B) is true, there is a whole range of social properties that we ascribe in the course of our lives, like being a mayor, opening a session of Parliament, voting, cashing a cheque, being a prison (a social property true of some buildings), for which no reductive analysis in terms of mental properties like believing and expecting is possible, since mental properties adequate for the analysis (if any; this is a moot point, given my first argument about variability) will themselves presuppose the existence of social properties of the same sort. I think that there is an important class of social properties which could not be reductively identified with the mental, even if it could be identified with it, because at least some of the mental properties associated with the application of each such social property must themselves be beliefs or expectations about the instancing of strongly social action types. No commitment to social properties is thereby escaped by the identification; hence, it cannot be reductive. J.W.N. Watkins describes approvingly Keynes's theory: 'At the heart of his *General Theory* Keynes placed "three fundamental psychological factors, namely, the psychological propensity to consume, the psychological attitude to liquidity and the psychological expectation of future yield

126

from capital-assets".'[19] Whatever form of individualism this is, it is certainly consistent with the existence of irreducible social properties, since some of the mental or psychological properties that Keynes mentions themselves presuppose the existence of strongly social properties.

Appendix to Chapter 3

In a brief, but perceptive, discussion of methodological individualism, Steven Lukes classifies properties predicable of human individuals on a 'continuum of . . . what one might call the most non-social to the most social.'[1] Lukes provides a list, which I reproduce below, which presumably highlights various important points on that continuum:

   (i)   genetic make-up; brain-states,
  (ii)   aggression; gratification; stimulus-response,
 (iii)   co-operation; power; esteem,
 (iv)   cashing cheques; saluting; voting.

In the ensuing discussion, Lukes makes it clear that properties of type (i) and type (ii) are examples of non-social properties. Of type (iii), he has this to say:

> Propositions incorporating only predicates of type (iii) do have a minimal social reference; they presuppose a social context in which certain actions, social relations, and/or mental states are picked out and given a particular significance (which makes social relations of a certain sort count as 'co-operative', which makes certain social positions count as positions of 'power' and a certain set of attitudes count as 'esteem'). They still do not presuppose or entail any particular propositions about any particular form of group or institution.

According to Lukes, it is only predicates of type (iv) which are 'maximally social', since propositions incorporating them 'presuppose and sometimes directly entail propositions about particular types of group and institution'.

In some ways, Lukes's distinction is akin to mine. His type (iv) predicates are close in inspiration to my strongly social properties. He says of a type (iv) predicate that propositions incorporating them entail propositions about a group or institution; I said, of strongly social properties, that the nested system of beliefs and expectations associated with them include beliefs and expectations about the instantiation of a social property. I prefer my account, because it frees the characterisation of 'maximally social' properties from questions about the individuation of groups and institutions. On both of our accounts, a property like saluting is 'maximally' or 'strongly' social. Lukes holds that it is maximally social, on the grounds that it entails a proposition about the (existence of the) institution of saluting; I say that saluting is a strongly social property because its application entails a nested system of beliefs and expectations, which will include beliefs and expectations about flags, patriotism, and so on. It seems that the only sense of 'institution' which will make Lukes's account plausible is a very broad one indeed, in which there is an institution of doing something (like an institution of saluting) just in case there are widespread and mutually interlocking beliefs and expectations. For this reason, I prefer my account of strongly or maximally social properties.

But Lukes's type (iii) predicates are quite different from my weakly social properties. To begin with, I dispute whether two of his examples, esteeming and having power, are examples of social properties at all, even in a weak or minimal sense. Power can be had by a person over an object. Esteeming something is a psychological property. One can esteem ability, and can esteem a theory useless. Neither of these uses of 'esteem' denotes a social property. I do not dispute, of course, that both power and esteem can have a social application, and it might even be that the social application of these two properties is their most frequent and interesting application. So, whereas there can be social power and social esteem, neither esteeming nor having power over are themselves social properties at all. On the other hand, Lukes's example of co-operating is a bona fide example of a social property.

Examples apart, Lukes's account of what it is for a property to be minimally social is not helpful. Taken literally, his account seems to be this: a property P is minimally social only if its application presupposes or entails that there is a social context such that in that social context certain (social?) actions, social relations, social positions, or mental attitudes count as those of which P is true (or, perhaps, 'are given a particular significance', although this is vague).

If this is Lukes's account of a minimally social property, it is not of much help. It uses in the analysans the ideas of a social context, a social relation, a social position, and perhaps the idea of a social action. These are themselves examples of either minimally or maximally social properties. If they are examples of minimally social properties of type (iii), the account of what it is for a property to be minimally social is circular. If his account is to escape circularity, he could use only strongly or maximally social properties of type (iv) in the analysans of a property P's being a minimally social property. But this would surely be an unhappy result; we ought to be able to say in what a property's being minimally social consists without using the idea of a maximally social property. This is especially desirable, given Lukes's very broad use of the idea of an institution. Lukes's use of 'institution' itself seems explicable, at least in part, by means of minimally social properties, or beliefs and expectations about minimally social properties.

CHAPTER 4

Methodological individualism

I construed metaphysical individualism as a thesis about what irreducible sorts of entities or properties there are. Methodological individualism (hereafter, 'm.i.') is not a doctrine about either of these matters. It is a doctrine about explanation. It asserts that, ultimately, everything that happens or occurs can be explained without recourse to social entities or social properties (as with metaphysical individualism, we can discern two possible variants of methodological individualism, one only about social properties, the other about both social properties and social entities). Because of a particular view about scientific explanation that some philosophers hold, methodological individualism is often formulated as a view about theory reduction, viz. the reduction of social science to psychology. It is important not to lose sight of the fact that it is, first and foremost, a doctrine about explanation, it being an open question, at least for the purposes of this book, how reduction and explanation are related, or indeed how deduction and explanation are related.

The central insight of m.i. is that, in some sense, there is an explanatory asymmetry between the non-social and the social. In some sense, the former can explain the latter in a way in which the latter cannot explain the former. As stated, this is a vague thought. The purpose of this chapter will be to make this vague thought about the explanatory priority or primacy of the non-social over the social precise enough to permit its evaluation. I do not claim that there is only one way in which this can be done, but only that in this chapter I formulate and consider one way in which this vague thought can and has been given more specific content. No doubt the reader will be able to think of other ways which I do not discuss.

Some preliminary remarks on explanation

My own view is that methodological individualism has never been stated with enough clarity and precision to permit its proper evaluation. One claim of this chapter is that I do state it clearly and precisely, at least in one plausible formulation. Even if the reader disagrees with my own negative evaluation of m.i., I hope that he will think that the work of developing a terminology which permits the careful formulation of m.i. has independent worth and merit. Perhaps doing this will allow that reader the more clearly to understand why he thinks that m.i. is true.

Discussions of m.i. typically fail to state explicitly the assumptions they are making about explanation in general. This is unfortunate, since m.i. is a thesis about a proper subset of all the explanations there are. This chapter is not about explanation *per se*. However, in this section, I hope both to make my assumptions about explanation clear, and to establish a terminology which will permit a precise and perspicuous formulation of a version of m.i.

I (tentatively) take (correct) explanation to be a two-place relation, true of ordered pairs of objects. The first of any such ordered pair I call (for want of a more apt expression) 'an explanans-entity'; the second I call 'an object of explanation'. Explanans-entities explain objects of explanation. Some may believe that the explanation relation is not completely expressed in the form 'x explains y', since they may take it to be a three-placed relation, 'person p explains y by means of x'. They may consider that the relation is true of ordered triplets of objects: persons, objects of explanation, explanans-entities. Persons explain objects of explanation by means of explanans-entities. I would not wish necessarily to resist this point. For those attracted by it, let my discussion which follows count as a partial discussion of two of the arguments of this three-placed relation.

The explanation relation in which I am interested by no means covers the whole field of explanation. It is, for example, generally agreed that one can sometimes explain what something is merely by offering an appropriate re-description of it. I might explain to someone what it is that is on my desk simply by saying that it is a ceremonial ram's horn. There is, however, an intuitive contrast between descriptive and non-descriptive explanation, or between describing and explaining proper, and although the former has a worthy place in the methodology of social science, it is only the latter in which I am interested. So too, some philosophers believe that there is a distinctive kind of explanation called 'philosophical explanation', perhaps an explanation of how something is possible. There are mathematical explanations, e.g. an explanation of why some mathematical theorem is true. But I deliberately exclude these cases of explanation from treatment here.

We also speak of how-explanations, and realist philosophers of science tend to make much of them. In my view, this is not a distinctive kind of explanation at all. To explain how something happened is to single out a special fragment from an explanation of why something happened. Sometimes it is obvious that one thing explains another only mediately or remotely. To ask for an explanation of how the second thing occurred, or how the first explains the second, is to ask for the more immediate explanation of the second, itself presumably to be explained by the first thing.

Given the way in which I have construed the explanation relation, three questions about explanation immediately arise. First, what is the nature of the explanation relation itself? Second, what sorts of things are explanans-entities? Third, what sorts of things are objects of explanation? The three questions concern the relation, its domain, and its range.

Objects of explanation and explanans-entities

What are the objects of explanation and explanans-entities, the relata of the explanation relation (at least for the explanation relation as restricted by my earlier remarks)? There seem to be two obvious possibilities: linguistic items and non-linguistic items. However, the reader might do well to consider Peter Achinstein's 'The object of explanation', for a critique of these two possibilities and the presentation of a third.[1]

Philosophers use 'explanans' and 'explanandum' (and their plurals, 'explanantia' and 'explananda') to refer to linguistic items, usually to sentences, which satisfy certain formal and other requirements. This is, of course, entirely unobjectionable, but some philosophers also believe that the explanation relation holds between explanantia and explananda, i.e. between linguistic items. This is controversial. For example, Donald Davidson says that: 'Explanations typically relate statements, not events.'[2]

It seems to me to be evident that it is not such linguistic items that we seek to explain, but rather whatever it is that those linguistic items are about. Indeed, I am not at all confident that I can understand the view that what is explained in an explanation is a sentence (or statement or proposition). 'Plato explained the sentence (or even, the *true* sentence) "Socrates died" ' sounds elliptical either for 'Plato explained the meaning of the sentence "Socrates died" ', which is of course not what is intended, or for 'Plato explained why the sentence "Socrates died" is true'. In the latter case, what Plato explained was why Socrates died, and this is surely to explain some non-linguistic item, an event, phenomenon, fact, or whatever, and not a linguistic item.

I am encouraged in this view by noting that philosophers whose official view it is that we explain sentences slip into speaking in other ways. Thus, Hempel and Oppenheim say: 'By the explanandum we understand the sentence describing the phenomenon to be explained.'[3] Whatever it is that we explain, it is typically a non-linguistic item. For ease of exposition, I sometimes lapse into speaking of an explanans explaining an explanandum. I take this to be an entirely derivative locution, and would ask the reader to take this as elliptical for 'the explanans-entity which the explanans is about explaining the object of explanation which the explanandum is about'. Explanans-entities explain objects of explanation. The relation of being the correct explanation of, then, is not in the first instance a relation between sentences, or sets thereof, but between non-linguistic items (in some sense yet to be decided).

What metaphysical sort of non-linguistic item are objects of explanation and explanans-entities? One might be forgiven for thinking that the explanation relation held between events, or anyway that the second relatum of the relation could be a particular event (I omit for the present the case of explaining laws). This thought might be reinforced by considering such a locution as:

(1) Jack's falling down explains Jack's breaking his crown.

What could be more non-linguistic, more in the world, than particular or token events? (1) appears to assert that the token event of Jack's falling down explains the token event of Jack's breaking his crown.

But such appearances would be misleading. First, we never explain just token events, but (as Hempel puts it) 'the object of . . . explanation in every branch of empirical science is always the occurrence of an event of a certain kind.'[4] Hempel's remark might get us to construe the object of explanation as a token-event-under-a-description, but this construal would still not take us far enough away from token events.

In empirical science, we are often not interested in explaining a token event at all (even assuming that this is possible), even a token event under a description. Rather, we often wish to explain why an event of some kind occurred. That is, we may be uninterested in explaining why this token event rather than some other token event of the same kind occurred, and interested only in explaining the fact that some token event or other of that kind occurred. At least sometimes, it is *facts* that we explain, and no account of the metaphysics of explanation can dispense with facts. I therefore take the relata of the explanation relation to be facts.

Given my previous dismissal of linguistic items as the relata of the explanation relation, it will come as no surprise that I regard facts as a metaphysical sort of non-linguistic item. There are numerous discussions in the literature about whether facts have a linguistic status or a non-linguistic status. Since the matter will not be pursued here, I refer the reader to those discussions.[5] Although I construe facts as non-linguistic, nothing in my subsequent discussion of m.i. depends on this. The central notion I will need will be that of an explanatory chain, which is a chain of facts. The notion is equally usable for my purposes in whichever way one regards facts.

There are many interesting questions about the metaphysics of facts which I here eschew, for instance questions of their individuation and their identity conditions. I do not think that one can fully decide issues about the extensionality or the non-extensionality of the sentence, 'the fact that p explains the fact that q', unless one is clear about the metaphysics of facts. There is no doubt though that substitution of sentences with the same truth value for the contained sentences, and substitution of co-extensive predicates for the predicates in the contained sentences, may alter the truth value of the whole.

I take the canonical form of the explanation relation, then, to be: the fact that p explains the fact that q. (1) is better expressed as:

(2)   The fact that Jack fell down explains the fact that
       Jack broke his crown.

(2) has at least four possible disambiguations, depending on whether the first and second of the facts mentioned are construed as particular or general facts, as I explain that distinction in the next paragraph. I do not restrict the facts that can be objects of explanation to facts about events. One might also explain the fact that a particular object has a certain property or the fact that there is an object with a certain property.

Let's classify facts, then, into three sorts. A fact is a particular fact if it has or entails something with this form: object o or token event e is P. A fact is general if it has or entails something with this form: there is some object or token event of type or kind P. A fact is a universal fact if it has or entails something of this form: any object or token event which is P is Q. It is because we sometimes explain general and universal facts that the objects of explanation at least sometimes cannot be token events, as (1) might suggest. More strongly, I would say that the objects of explanation are always facts; the closest an explanation can get to particular objects or token events is to be an explanation of a particular fact.

In any explanation of a general or particular fact, the explanans-entity includes general or particular facts. Some philosophers assert that every such explanans must also include a set of universal hypotheses or universally quantified laws. In terms of my terminology, this is equivalent to the assertion that every such explanans-entity includes universal facts as well as particular or general facts. I believe that this is true. But I would not wish to build this in as a requirement, for the purposes of this chapter. Someone might believe that one particular or general fact could explain another, without the addition of a universal fact. If there could be such a case, it would be true that derivability of explanandum from explanans would fail, but I do not intend to rule out, again for the purposes of this discussion of m.i., the possibility of full explanation in the absence of such deductive derivability. One might believe that one general or particular fact could explain another because of some immediately intelligible connection between the two general or particular facts, and in the absence of any universal fact connecting the kinds of things the particular or general facts are about. I am sceptical of this idea, but we need not decide it one way or another here.

Finally, I introduce the idea of an explanation or explanatory chain. Suppose some fact f_1 explains fact f_2, and fact f_2 explains fact f_3. If so, they form (part of) an explanation chain:

$$f_1 \to f_2 \to f_3$$

The arrow represents the explanation relation, such that the fact immediately to the left of the arrow explains the fact immediately to the right of the arrow. I do not assume that the explanation relation is transitive. I do not infer, therefore, that in any explanation chain, two facts between which one or more facts intervene themselves stand in the explanation relation to one another. For example, in the above diagram, I do not assume that f_1 explains f_3. I still need, however, some name for the relation that obtains between facts like f_1 and f_3. Consider, then, any two facts in an explanation chain between which one or more facts intervene. Of the fact further to the left, I shall say that it is an explanation-ancestor of the fact further to the right in the chain. Of the fact further to the right, I shall say that it is an explanation-descendant of the fact further to the left in the chain.

Speaking of explanation chains as unilinear involves a double simplification. First, as I indicated, most philosophers believe that a general or particular fact can only be explained by a conjunction of facts, at least one of which is a universal fact. Second, it typically (although not invariably) requires a plurality of general or particular facts (in addition to any universal facts) to explain one general or particular fact. That is, explanation chains are always backwards-branching, as the diagram below shows. To speak of an explanatory chain is an abstraction, by which we single out a unilinear explanatory thread from such a backwards-branching tree. The trees include all the general, particular, and universal facts required in the explanation of some object of explanation. In the diagram below, in addition to the symbols I have already used, the vertical line represents conjunction.

$$
\begin{array}{llll}
f_1 & & & \\
\,|\;\; & \to & f_3 & \\
f_2 & & \,|\;\; & \to & f_5 \\
& & f_4 & & \,|\;\; & \to \cdots \\
& & & & f_6
\end{array}
$$

$$\begin{array}{l} f_7 \\ \ldots \ldots \quad | \quad \rightarrow \quad f_9 \\ f_8 \quad | \quad \rightarrow \quad f_{11} \\ \quad \quad f_{10} \end{array}$$

From this tree, we can pick out one explanatory chain as: f_1 explains f_3 explains f_5 explains f_7 explains f_9 explains f_{11}. But f_2, f_4, f_6, f_8, and f_{10} have explanations too, and the more of this that is represented, the more like a tree the diagram would look. For ease of exposition, I speak of explanatory chains, but nothing in my argument depends on this. Explanatory chains are simply continuous threads of backwards-branching explanatory trees. The reader may wish to think of the relation I describe that obtains between two facts as the relation of partly explaining or the relation of being part of the explanation of. The relation of fully explaining is only to be found in explanatory trees, between the conjunction of facts to the left of an arrow and the fact to the right of the arrow.

Social facts

This chapter is about the explanation of social facts. Which facts are social facts? A universal fact is a universal social fact if either P or Q or both is a social property. A general fact is a general social fact if P is a social property. A particular fact is a particular social fact if *either* P is a social property *or* the object o or the event token e is a social object or social event token. (These characterisations of a social fact, and indeed of a fact generally, can easily be extended to cover the case of relational facts.)

If follows that, in the way in which I use the term, it is a social fact that La Guardia was mayor of New York, that the oldest building I have ever seen was a Minoan palace, and that France is a charter member of the United Nations. Some philosophers write as if the ascription of a social property to an individual or to a non-social object is not itself a social

139

fact; social facts for them, if particular, are always facts about social entities of some sort. For those philosophers, the first two of the three examples of a particular social fact I gave would not qualify for that status. There is no philosophical importance in using 'particular social fact' one way or another. It is only of philosophical importance to be clear and consistent about its use, and this, as we shall see in an appendix to this chapter, is precisely what the literature has not been.

Garfinkel on the objects of explanation

Alan Garfinkel claims that the objects of explanation are contrast spaces or equivalence classes of possible worlds.[6] His reason for thinking this is that when we ask a question like 'Why did Willy Sutton rob banks?', our question is implicitly contrastive. As it stands, not only is 'Why did Willy Sutton rob banks?' incomplete, but there is more than one way in which to complete it. There is, then, an ambiguity in the meaning of the question we are asking. We might be asking for an explanation of why he robbed banks rather than not rob at all, or we might be asking for an explanation of why he robbed banks rather than rob other things. So the two objects of explanation, on Garfinkel's view, are distinct. The first is: Sutton's robbing banks rather than not robbing at all. The second is: Sutton's robbing banks rather than robbing other things.

One can express Garfinkel's point using the terminology of facts, rather than equivalence classes of logically possible worlds. The two objects of explanation are general facts: first, the fact that there were some bank robbings by Sutton rather than there being no robbings by Sutton at all; second, the fact that there were some bank robbings by Sutton rather than there being some robbings of other things by Sutton. Garfinkel's thesis can be expressed thus: objects of explanation are always contrastive facts, in the sense that they are facts that one alternative obtained rather than some other alternative. I dispute this thesis.

140

Consider the first, allegedly contrastive fact, that there were some bank robbings by Sutton rather than no robbings at all by Sutton. If this is a genuinely contrastive fact, it must have more content to it than does the (allegedly incomplete) fact that there were some bank robbings by Sutton. What more content could it have? If it is true that there were some bank robbings by Sutton, it follows logically that it is false that there were no bank robbings at all by Sutton. That is, the second 'bit' of the supposedly contrastive fact, -rather-than-no-robbings by Sutton, is logically redundant. To refer to the fact as the fact that there were some bank robbings by Sutton rather than no robbings at all by Sutton is a pleonasm for the simpler description of the same fact, that there were some bank robbings by Sutton. Far from the simpler description being incomplete, the fuller description in otiose.

Why is the fact, of which both the simpler and fuller descriptions are true, not a contrastive fact? The answer is that if Garfinkel were correct about this, his argument could be construed as a general argument against the possibility of any non-contrastive facts whatever, whether or not they were the objects of explanation. Consider any intuitively non-contrastive fact, for example the fact that some material object has some physical property. The same fact can always be pleonastically described as the fact that that material object has that property rather than fails to have that property. If the ability to offer such a pleonastic description of the fact was a criterion of the fact's being contrastive, it would be impossible for there to be any non-contrastive facts at all. I conclude that the fact that there were some bank robbings by Sutton is not a contrastive fact.

What about the second, allegedly contrastive fact, that there were some bank robbings by Sutton rather than robbings of other things by him? Suppose that I can explain the fact that Willy Sutton robbed banks, that is, the fact that there were some bank robbings by Sutton. It is true that in explaining that fact, I will not thereby explain the fact, if it is one, that he did not rob other things. He might, after all, have robbed banks *and* robbed other things. But suppose it is true that criminals tend to specialise and rob things of only one sort. If I conjoin this to my explanation of why he robbed banks, I will then have managed to explain why he did not rob other things. There are *two* non-contrastive facts here, not *one* contrastive fact: the fact that there were some bank robbings by Sutton, and the fact that there were no robbings by Sutton of other things. An explanation of the first will not, by itself, be an explanation of the second.

I claim that if one can explain why Sutton robbed banks, then one has explained, given the addition about robbers' specialisation, why Sutton did not rob other things. I conjecture that any intuition that one may have that all of this might still not be sufficient to explain why he did not rob other things arises from a not uncommon confusion about precisely what a specific explanation does explain. For instance, we might say that we have explained why Willy Sutton was a bank robber, by giving a story about his deprived background and circumstances. If this explanatory story does explain anything, it can only explain, at best, why Willy Sutton robbed something. It will not, on its own, explain why he robbed banks.[7] In order to explain the latter, we will need an additional explanatory story about the sort of institution banks are and how they were choice targets for robbers.

There are, then, at least three non-contrastive facts, with varying degrees of specificity. There is the fact that there were some robbings by Sutton, the fact that there were some bank robbings by Sutton, and the fact that there were no robbings of other things by him. An explanation of the first will be insufficient, by itself, to explain the second, and an explanation of the second will be insufficient, by itself, to explain the third. There is no need, in the case of explaining any of these objects of explanation, to suppose that we are explaining a contrastive fact.

The explanation relation

Of the three questions concerning explanation that I indicated, let us consider finally the question of the nature of the explanation relation itself. It would be desirable to discuss m.i. in such a way that the arguments about it were neutral with regard to this issue, or anyway were neutral as far as this is possible.

I do not know, and hence do not wish to be committed about, what conditions are both necessary and sufficient for the truth of 'the fact that p explains the fact that q'. But I do want to discuss and comment upon a controversy regarding *one* of the conditions necessary for the truth of 'the fact that p explains the fact that q'.

As far as I can see, there are three views one might hold about this necessary condition for explanation. First, there is the deductivist view, to which I subscribe, according to which a necessary condition for an adequate or sound complete explanation is that an explanans-entity can explain an object of explanation *only if* the explanans about that entity logically entails the explanandum about that object of explanation. A deductivist can, of course, admit that there can be partial or incomplete explanations, or explanation sketches, or whatever, in which explanans does not entail explanandum. What is distinctive about his view is his insistence that there is but one kind of complete explanation, namely one in which the description of the object of explanation is entailed by the explanans. Some Popperians adhere to the deductivist view from a general scepticism concerning the idea of inductive support, but my own adherence to deductivism springs from no such motive.

The other two views represent different degrees of permissiveness with regard to non-deductive relations. The second view is the 'orthodox' Hempelian one, on which a necessary condition for an adequate or sound, complete or full explanation of an object of explanation by an explanans-entity is that the explanans about that entity *either* logically entails *or* inductively supports the explanandum about that object.[8] The insertion of the word 'complete' is essential, in order to distinguish this view from the deductivist view, which also accepts partial or incomplete explanations that do not conform to deductive standards. The idea behind this orthodox view is that there is a distinctive way in which an occurrence can be fully or completely explained, in addition to the way accepted by the deductivist. This way of fully or completely explaining can sometimes be achieved when an explanandum is inductively supported or made probable by an explanans.

Finally, there is the third, 'unorthodox' view which states that there can be a sound or adequate complete explanation of an object of explanation by an explanans-entity even when the explanandum about that object is improbable given the explanans about that entity.[9]

The unorthodox view is put by van Fraassen, among others:

The half-life of uranium U^{238} is (4.5). 10^9 years. Hence the probability that a given small enough sample of uranium will emit radiation in a specified small interval of time is low. Suppose, however, that it does. We still say that atomic physics explains this, the explanation being that this material was uranium, which has a certain atomic structure, and hence is subject to spontaneous decay. Indeed, atomic physics explains many more examples of events of a very low probability. (p. 105)

Atomic physics does not *explain* such events. Rather, it asserts that the occurrence of such events is, at least on current theory, inexplicable. My argument for the contention that an explanans-entity cannot explain an object of explanation when the explanandum about that object is improbable, given the explanans about that entity, is partly taken from D.H. Mellor.[10]

There is a necessary condition for the adequacy of explanation that can be traced back to remarks by Plato: one explanans cannot explain two contradictory explananda. This requirement can be supported by the following line of thought. In a successful explanation, the explanandum must be true. This is too obvious usually to be mentioned in accounts of explanation. The point is that we explain what happened or failed to happen, so that we relate, in some way now under discussion, the true statement that something happened or failed to happen, to an explanans. No account of the relation between explanans and explanandum

144

which permitted us to 'explain' a false explanandum would be worth much, for we would thereby be explaining some object of explanation which never occurred!

But now consider any statement 'p' and its denial 'not-p'. One of the two must be false. If an explanans could explain both of two contradictory explananda, it could explain a false explanandum. Therefore, no explanans can explain both of two contradictory explananda.

Now, return to van Fraassen's case. Let 'p' be the statement that this sample of uranium emits radiation in the specified time interval. He claims that this is explained by the fact that this material is uranium, which has a certain atomic structure and half-life, in spite of the fact that the emission of radiation in the specified period is highly improbable, given those facts. Now consider its denial, 'not-p', which asserts that it is not the case that this sample of uranium will emit radiation in the specified time interval. Note that the same explanans which was held to explain 'p' (but on which 'p' was improbable) makes 'not-p' probable.

Surely, the fact that this uranium has a certian atomic structure with a certain half-life can explain the probable occurrence of its failing to emit radiation if it can explain the improbable occurrence of its emitting radiation. But this would mean that the same explanans could explain both 'p' and 'not-p', which contravenes the above-mentioned condition for the adequacy of explanation. Therefore, either those facts fail to explain the probable non-emission of radiation or they fail to explain the improbable emission of radiation; the only reasonable choice is to say that they fail to explain the latter, despite van Fraassen's claims. I conclude that it is false that there can be a sound explanation of an object of explanation by an explanans-entity when the explanandum about that object is improbable, given the explanans about that entity.

If the atomic facts fail to explain the improbable emission of radiation, it certainly does not follow, from my argument that those facts cannot explain both the improbable emission and the probable non-emission, that they do successfully fully explain the probable non-emission of radiation. Can some explanans-entity completely explain an object of explanation when the explanandum about that object is made probable given the explanans about that entity?

I must say that I find the 'orthodox' view, on which an explanans can fully or completely explain an explanandum in some non-deductive way if, *inter alia*, the explanandum is merely probable given the explanans, singularly unattractive and unintuitive. I find it difficult to account for its wide acceptance. The orthodox view is that there are two different or distinct ways in which an explanans can fully or completely explain an explanandum: a deductive way and an inductive way. The orthodox theorist need not hold that this fact is sufficient to render the term 'explanation' ambiguous. He need not believe that there are two distinct meanings of the term. But he must believe that there are these two different kinds of complete explanation.

That there is something which can be called a complete, inductive explanation seems to be particularly implausible in the case of explanation of particular facts. I do not deny, of course, that we sometimes say, truly, such things as John's smoking explains his getting lung cancer. But to say this, I hold, is to give a partial or incomplete explanation of the only type of complete explanation of a particular event there is, in which explanans logically entails explanandum. Such an incomplete explanation of John's getting lung cancer is a good explanation only if there are other true premisses, perhaps unknown, such that when conjoined with the premiss that John smokes, logically entail that John gets lung cancer. If this were not so, then to say that John got lung cancer because he smoked could not even be (as it sometimes is) an incomplete or partial explanation of his getting lung cancer. A fact can incompletely explain another fact only when the first fact is a member of a set of facts which completely explains the second fact.

I find myself in agreement with both Michael Scriven and William Dray on this point. Scriven, for example, says that: 'Statistical statements are too weak – they abandon the hold on the individual case. . . . An event can rattle around inside a network of statistical laws',[11] and Dray repeats Scriven's observation as a way of signalling his assent to this.[12] Hempel's own reply to this line of criticism is

METHODOLOGICAL INDIVIDUALISM

concerned only with pointing out the inconsistency of admitting that the law that the flipping of a regular coin yields heads with a probability $\frac{1}{2}$ can explain why the number of heads in an actual empirical series of flippings fell between 4900 and 5100, while denying that there can be an inductive or probabilistic explanation of a particular event.[13] This is an inconsistency, because the first admission is an admission that there *can* be an explanation when the explanandum is merely probable given the explanans, which is what is being denied in the case of the explanation of a particular event.[14] But what Hempel has no reply to is a consistent opponent, who denies that there is *any* complete, non-deductive explanation being produced either in the case of the particular event or in the case of the particular series of flippings.

Perhaps the following observations, while not 'proving' that there can be no such thing as a full or complete non-deductive explanation, will at least serve to make the view more credible. Suppose we know that only n per cent (where n is more than 50 but less than 100) of smokers get lung cancer. The orthodox view holds that this can provide us with a full but non-deductive explanation of why John, who smoked, got lung cancer. Suppose we believed that 'n per cent of smokers get lung cancer' was irreducibly statistical. If it were, and if John smoked, it would still be, on my deductivist view, rational to predict that he will get cancer. I do not, of course, conflate explanations with arguments generally. However, in the case at hand, the existence of the good inductive argument, whose premises are that n per cent of smokers get lung cancer and that John smokes, and whose conclusion is that John gets lung cancer, *explains* why it is rational to believe or predict that he will get lung cancer (and does *not* explain the fact that John got lung cancer, if he did), because the existence of the good inductive argument *entails* that this is a rational bet (at least on one account of inductive argument).

But this is not to admit, in the case in which we thought that the law connecting smoking and lung cancer was irreducibly statistical, that we have an explanation of why John gets lung cancer, if he does. Indeed, if 'n per cent of smokers get lung cancer' is irreducibly statistical, then I hold that there can be in principle no possibility of explaining why John gets lung cancer. If determinism were true, we could always in principle obtain explanations for the particular changes or failures of change that occur, because we could always in principle deduce explananda from explanantia. If determinism is false, and derivability of what happens from what has happened plus universally quantified laws fails, then explicability of particular happenings (as well as explicability of why a particular empirical series of happenings turned out in some way) also fails.

Here I part company with William Dray, who thinks that the non-determined is explicable. Dray speaks of a 'rational explanation', appropriate in the study of history, which is meant, presumably, to be distinct in its logical form from both an explanation in which explanans entails explanandum and an explanation in which the explanandum is probable given the explanans. Dray's rational explanations make use of neither universally quantified nor statistical laws. Dray's idea is that, in the light of the explanans, the action of the agent mentioned in the explanandum is made 'intelligible', shown to be a 'reasonable' thing to do or have done. Dray asserts that 'the rational model of explanation . . . shows a way in which explanation can be given in history which is logically compatible with indeterminism regarding human actions'.[15]

A difficulty I have with Dray's view is the apparent tension between his rejection of probabilistic explanation of particular happenings on the one hand and his acceptance of rational explanation on the other. Rational explanation, if it could be said to explain anything at all, could only account for the fact that some action was the sort of thing an agent might well have done on some occasion. Many actions might all be 'reasonable' or 'intelligible' from an agent's point of view on some particular occasion. Since that is the case, a rational explanation could not possibly explain why an agent took the single course of action he did, from the various 'reasonable' alternatives open to him. If an event can rattle around in a network of statistical laws, so much more can an event rattle around inside a network of sensible or reasonable things the agent might have done. If the first rattling is a reason for rejecting inductive explanation of individual cases, then the second rattling would be a reason for rejecting Dray's rational explanation of an agent's acting as he did.

So I reject the orthodox view that an explanans-entity can fully or completely explain an object of explanation when the explanandum about that object is merely probable given the explanans about that entity. The orthodox view (and indeed Dray) tries to retain explicability even if forced to surrender determinism; on my view, determinism and explicability stand or fall together.

I think that many readers will not find my views on the explanation relation convincing. In my discussion of m.i., I attempt to state and criticise the doctrine in a way that does not presuppose the deductivist view of explanation. It is not always easy to do this, because so much of the literature about m.i. assumes without argument the deductivist account of explanation. This arises from the fact, in part, that there is a tendency to concentrate on the special case of explanation of one science by another by deriving the first deductively from the second (plus bridge laws). As far as possible, I try not to restrict my discussion by deductivist assumptions about explanation, in spite of the fact that I think these assumptions are true. I do not similarly make allowances for the third, unorthodox view, since I take myself to have given reasons sufficient for its dismissal.

I presume that it is uncontroversial that the explanation relation is irreflexive and asymmetric: nothing can explain itself, and nothing can be explained by that which it explains. It is also clear that the explanation relation is not intransitive: sometimes if one thing explains a second and the second explains a third, it is true that the first does explain the third.[16] Is the explanation relation, then, transitive or non-transitive? This is, I think, more controversial, and it is not easy to answer it, in the absence of a full analysis of explanation, giving conditions necessary and sufficient for explanation, and this is a task I have here forsworn. The safest course, then, is to conduct my discussion of m.i. on the assumption that the relation is non-transitive. This only serves to make my argument more difficult; if the relation were transitive, I would simply have an easier time of it. I could eliminate certain complications in my formulation of m.i. as unnecessary.

Methodological individualism

I now come to the central purpose of this chapter. As I said at the beginning, the initial discussion of explanation was intended merely to establish a clear and perspicuous terminology in which to state m.i. I also remind the reader that the version of m.i. that I here formulate is not intended to be the only version of such a doctrine that there might be. My formulation is only meant to capture one prevalent and plausible doctrine that can be found, commonly, in the literature about m.i.

Here are two statements of m.i. which will provide us with such a plausible version of m.i. The first is by Macdonald and Pettit, the second by John Watkins.

> The idea is that for any event which the collectivist holds to be inexplicable except by reference to groups or practices, the orthodox [individualist] conception will suppose that there is a perfectly individualistic explanation by reference to the beliefs and desires of the appropriate agents.[17]

> There may be unfinished or half-way explanations of large-scale social phenomena . . . ; but we shall not have arrived at rock-bottom explanations of such large-scale phenomena until we have deduced an account of them from statements about the dispositions, beliefs, (physical) resources, and interrelations of individuals.[18]

We can extract an initial statement of m.i. by slightly modifying and generalising these two claims. First, in Watkins's characterisation of m.i., let us replace 'deduced an account of them from statements about' by 'explained them by means of'. This reformulation will permit us to capture a version of m.i., untied to the deductivist commitments about explanation that I earlier described. Second, methodological individualists typically write as if the 'rock-bottom' explanans-entities are restricted to psychological facts about agents ('beliefs and desires'). Watkins adds to these psychological facts, facts about physical resources and interrelations of individuals. This is a point we shall need to return to, and certainly a central claim of m.i. is the importance of psychological explanations of social facts. Let us, for the present, not restrict these explanans-entities to psychological facts. The doctrine we are trying to characterise is committed only to the explanatory priority of the non-social over the social. Therefore, we shall speak of these explanans-entities, which rock-bottom explanantia are about, as including no *social* facts, leaving it open for now precisely what it is they are about. From this perspective, Watkins's addition of 'physical resources' to the list presents no difficulty. However, the only 'interrelations of individuals' which are acceptable as what rock-bottom explanantia can be about, according to methodological individualism, must be psychological or physical interrelations. It seems obvious that if social relations were to be included, the doctrine would be incapable of giving any sense whatever to the idea of the explanatory priority of the non-social over the social.

Third, Macdonald and Pettit say that, for any explanation in which the explanans mentions anything social, there is another explanation of the same explanandum which does not mention anything social. This overlooks the obvious possibility that, rather than *replace* the first, social explanans with an alternative, second explanans, which is non-social, we may prefer to retain the first, social explanans, but then in turn explain it by means of a second, non-social explanans. Our characterisation of m.i. should allow for both possibilities.

Fourth, Watkins says that the problematic objects of explanation are 'large-scale social phenomena'. D.H. Mellor says that the problematic object of explanation is 'the social behaviour of groups'.[19] These objects of explanation do not include just the same things (that is, facts about the one are

151

not identical with facts about the other). Now, it is quite impossible to evaluate m.i. unless we are clear both about the explananda and about the explanantia that fall within its claims. Sometimes we give *social* explanations of objects of explanation when the latter are neither facts about large-scale social phenomena nor facts about the social behaviour of groups. For instance, I might explain someone's increased nervousness as the result of the outbreak of a war or economic recession. Or I might explain soil erosion as the result of the agricultural policy of some short-sighted government. The methodological individualists' claim ought surely to cover these sorts of examples as well, in which the objects of explanation are non-social facts.

Let us, then, put these four points together, in order to obtain a first formulation of m.i. (we shall need to improve upon it later). Let e be any explanation whatever, and p be its explanans and q its explanandum. Perhaps methodological individualism can be expressed by means of a five-horned lemma:

(1)   *Either* (a) Both p and q are about non-social facts.
      Or (b) q is about a social fact, but p is about a non-social fact.
      Or (c) p is about a social fact (whether or not q is about a social fact), and there is another explanation e' such that q is the explanandum in e' and there is another explanans of q in e', r, and r is about a non-social fact.
      Or (d) p is about a social fact (whether or not q is about a social fact), and there is another explanation e' such that p is the explanandum in e' and there is an explanans of p in e', r, and r is about a non-social fact.
      Or (e) p is about a social fact (whether or not q is about a social fact), and there is an explanatory chain, in which the facts mentioned by p and q figure, such that some explanatory ancestor of the fact mentioned by p is a non-social fact.

(1) makes a claim about all explanations whatsoever. It says that, in any explanation, either the explanans-entity is a non-social fact (the first and second lemmas), or, in case it is a social fact, either it is replaceable by a non-social fact (the third lemma), or it is itself explainable by means of a non-social fact (the fourth lemma), or it is an explanatory-descendant of a non-social fact (the fifth lemma). Aside from some doubts I have about (3) – why does the existence of an alternative non-social explanation of q make the non-social explanation in any sense primary relative to q's social explanation? – (1) *seems* able to make precise the vague idea of the explanatory priority of the non-social over the social.

The requirements of (1) apply to each fact in the conjunction of such facts that jointly explain some other fact, and to each such fact in the conjunction of facts that jointly explain each fact in the first conjunction, and so on. That is, as explanatory trees branch backwards, the requirements embodied in (1) apply to each branch, and to each branch of that branch, and so on. But we overlook this complication for ease of exposition.

It is important to be clear about what (1) does *not* require. In particular, (1) does not assert that these social-fact-free explanantia can dispense with the existence of social properties, even with irreducible social properties. Examples that supporters of m.i. adduce as acceptable, non-social explanans-entities, fulfilling the requirements of (1), are (facts about) such things as beliefs and desires of agents, and, in giving content to those beliefs and desires, they make liberal use of social properties to describe the contents of agents' psychological states. In chapter 3, I quoted Watkins's approval of Keynes's strategy of basing his economic theory on 'three fundamental psychological factors, namely the psychological propensity to consume, the psychological attitude to liquidity, and the psychological expectation of future yield from capital-assets'. An example in Macdonald and Pettit that I discussed in the first chapter was that of the beliefs and desires of peasants regarding monetary rewards and the commodities they could thereby acquire. The full sentence from Mellor, a part of which I quoted above, asserts: 'the social behaviour of groups *can* be so derived (and hence explained), from how people think and feel about social facts.'[20] All of these attributions of psychological properties to persons presuppose the existence of social properties (the property of being a social fact, a commodity, a monetary reward, a capital asset), but they do not presuppose the existence of any particular, general, or universal social facts.

That is, the attribution of these psychological states or properties to agents, although it involves commitment to social properties, does not say or presuppose that anything has any of these social properties (or that some social property is universally connected with some other property). It is consistent with m.i., in any plausible version, that there are irreducible social properties, available to it in the description of the psychological states of individuals.

I should perhaps make it clear that I do not make these remarks in the spirit of criticism of m.i., but rather as a way of stating it in its most plausible form. No psychology which did not accept the existence of social properties as part of its theoretical repertoire and did not include social predicates in its vocabulary as a means of describing the content of agents' beliefs and desires would be sufficiently rich to be an even initially plausible explainer of social life.

Although this is not intended as a criticism of m.i., it can be used to criticise an argument found in the writings of Karl Popper.[21] Popper rejects a view he calls 'psychologism': the idea that 'social laws must ultimately be reducible to psychological laws'. One of his two arguments against psychologism is that it assumes that social rules and institutions 'can be traced back to a state when their introduction was dependent solely upon psychological factors, or more precisely, when it was independent of any established social institutions. Psychologism is thus forced, whether it likes it or not, to operate with the idea of a *beginning of society*, and with the idea of a human nature and a human psychology as they existed prior to society.'[22]

There is more than one thing wrong with this argument, but one of them is this. Popper assumes, quite without warrant, that the psychology necessary for explaining the social supposes human beings in a situation in which there are no social facts. This is certainly not so. The required psychology does not assume, on the face of it, that there are any social facts, but this is not the same thing as supposing that there are no social facts. Popper simply conflates not supposing that there are any social facts with supposing that there are no social facts. Indeed, since the required psychology makes free use of social properties in describing the content of agents' beliefs and desires, if psychologism did suppose that there are no social facts, it would be supposing that agents were subject to total illusion about the existence of society, at least at the time at which they were in those psychological states. That is, agents would believe such things as that monetary payments promised them certain rewards, that they could expect future yields from their capital-assets, and that certain social facts obtained, and yet none of those beliefs would be true (because society did not yet exist)! This is simply absurd, and disposes of one of Popper's arguments against psychologism. Even psychologism is not committed to any beginning of society, as Popper supposes.

Is (1) an adequate characterisation of m.i.?

Roughly speaking, what (1) says is that there is some explanation for every fact, or some explanatory ancestor for every fact (and *a fortiori* for every social fact), which is or includes only non-social facts. Now, despite this being the content often given to m.i., (1) by itself cannot possibly capture adequately the central insight of the explanatory priority of the non-social over the social

(1) did not assert that every social fact has *an explanation* in terms of only non-social facts. Let 'n' (with subscripts) represent non-social facts; let 's' (with subscripts) represent social facts. There may be explanation chains that look like this.

$$n_1 \rightarrow s_2 \rightarrow s_1$$

Since the explanation relation is non-transitive, s_2 has a non-

155

social explanation but s_1 may not have a non-social explanation. But even s_1 has a non-social explanatory ancestor, and we hoped that this thought might help to capture the idea of the explanatory priority of the non-social over the social (disregarding complications due to backwards-branching explanatory trees).

The idea of explanatory priority was that in some sense the explanatory capabilities of the social and the non-social were asymmetric: in some sense, the non-social could explain (or be the explanatory ancestor of) the social in a way in which the social could not explain (or be the explanatory ancestor) of the non-social. (1) insures that, going backwards in every explanatory chain, we will find some point at which the explanatory chain has become free of any social facts. We call that point in the chain 'social-fact-free'.

It is consistent with (1) that n_1 is explained by social fact s_3. Of course, if (1) is true, then s_3 has somewhere back in the explanatory chain, whether as its explanation or as an explanation ancestor, a further non-social fact. That is, somewhere back in the explanatory chain leading to s_3, there is another point in the chain which is wholly social-fact-free. But what is consistent with (1) is that, as one travels backwards along these explanatory chains, they repeatedly become social-fact-free at a point, with such social-fact-freeness continually disappearing and reappearing in a never-ending pattern. This would insure that every fact, and *a fortiori* every social fact, had *some* explanans-entity or *some* explanatory ancestor that was a non-social fact, yet it seems inconsistent with the central insight of m.i., the explanatory primacy of non-social facts over social facts.

Graphically, imagine that below is a fragment of an explanatory chain which continues backwards (i.e. to the left) indefinitely, repeating the same pattern as instanced by the fragment:

$$s_4 \rightarrow n_2 \rightarrow s_3 \rightarrow n_1 \rightarrow s_2 \rightarrow s_1$$

Explanations could consist of infinite chains or series of facts, with no first member. This is, I submit, not a far-fetched possibility at all. If explanation chains had this character, then for each point in the chain at which there was a social fact, there could be *some* earlier point in the chain at which there were only non-social facts, but there might be a still earlier point in the chain, prior to that social-fact-free point, at which social facts reappeared in the chain, and so on indefinitely.

Or perhaps explanatory chains might circle around, forming closed explanatory loops, embracing both social and non-social facts in a circular fashion. Both of these two possibilities seem consistent with (1). Much of the literature of m.i. is expressed in terms of 'bedrock' and 'ultimate' explanations, in contrast to 'half-way' explanations. I have no doubt that they intend to exclude these indefinitely reappearing social fact possibilities. What must we require in order to rule them out?

The second possibility is perhaps the less plausible of the two. We normally think of the explanation relation as irreflexive and asymmetric, as I have already indicated. Nothing can explain itself, and nothing can be explained by what it explains. Suppose fact f_1 explains fact f_2, fact f_2 explains fact f_3, and fact f_3 explains fact f_1, thus constituting a closed explanatory loop. If the explanation relation were transitive, we could infer that f_1 explained itself (offending the irreflexivity requirement), and that f_2 explains f_1 as well as f_1 explaining f_2 (offending the asymmetry requirement). But since I chose to remain uncommitted concerning the transitivity of the explanation relation, this argument is unavailable to me.

However, on the other hand, the relation of being the explanatory ancestor of is certainly a transitive relation. Moreover, it seems intuitive that no fact can be the explanatory ancestor of itself, and that no fact can be the explanatory ancestor of a fact which is its explanatory ancestor. So explanatory loops offend the asymmetry and irreflexivity requirements for the explanatory ancestor relation, and perhaps can be dismissed on those grounds.

The first possibility, infinite explanatory chains, seems genuine, or anyway no methodological individualist of whom I am aware has ever dismissed it. But since such an infinite explanatory chain with the character I described is consistent with (1), it must follow that (1) is too weak to fully capture the idea of explanatory primacy or priority.

My formulation of m.i. must be altered in some way to deal with the possibility of infinite chains with continually appearing, disappearing, and reappearing social-fact-freeness. There are two cases we will want our new formulation to cover, depending on whether explanatory chains are finite or infinite in length:

(2) If an explanatory chain is finitely long, it is sufficient, to insure the explanatory priority of the non-social, that the first member of the chain be a non-social fact.

(3) If an explanatory chain is infinitely long back-wards, then it is sufficient, to insure the explan-atory priority of the non-social, that there be *some* point on the chain with only non-social facts and such that *no* facts in the chain prior to that point (there will be an infinite number of them) are social facts.

Both ways of insuring the explanatory priority of non-social facts, depending on whether the chains are of finite or infinite length, can be summed up in the following, which I substitute for (1):

(4) For every explanatory chain, there is *some* point in the chain at which there are only non-social facts and such that either there are no facts prior to that point at all, *or*, if there are, no facts prior to that point are social facts.

(4) asserts that there is some point on every explanatory chain at which there are only non-social facts which *either* have no explanans-entities nor explanation ancestors at all, *or* anyway have none which are or include social facts.

The two cases, (2) and (3), together with the idea of explanatory loops, suggest parallels with various views in the theory of belief justification: foundationalism, coherence, and infinite regress theories. I do not mean that holding one sort of theory about explanation commits one to its cousin about the justification of belief. The comparison is meant only to illuminate the choices available concerning explanation. In his use of terms like 'ultimate' and 'bedrock', versus 'half-way', explanations, the methodological individualist might seem to be opting for a sort of explanatory foundationalist doctrine for the social sciences, as if the 'ultimate' explanations of social facts that he will accept must themselves have no further explanation. But (3) makes it clear that a supporter of m.i. is not committed to explanatory foundationalism. (2) suggests a parallel with foundationalism, but (3) corresponds to an infinite regress theory. In the discussion that follows, I will continue using the expression 'ultimate explanation'. However, in using that expression, I do not mean that I regard m.i. as committed to explanatory foundationalism. An ultimate explanans, in the sense I intend, is any explanans that meets the requirements of either (2) or (3). Thus, some explanans might be ultimate, as far as m.i. is concerned, not because the fact it is about has no explanation at all, but because no social facts figure among its explanans-entity or its explanatory ancestors.

It may be that (3) strikes the reader as epistemologically suspect. How, someone might ask, could we ever know that no social facts reappeared in a chain going backwards from some point, since there must be an infinite number of facts that we should have to examine? If this were a genuine difficulty, it would be a difficulty for ever being in a position to know that m.i. was true (if there were infinite chains). But I think that that sort of objection to (3) would be specious. We can be practically certain that some non-social facts will have no social facts anywhere among the preceding infinity of facts (if there is one) that make up their explanatory ancestors. For example, if we could find, for every social fact, an explanans-entity or explanatory ancestor that was a fact only about the physical composition of the stars, then, even if the explanatory chain backwards from the facts about the stars were infinitely long, we could still justifiably conclude that (3) had been satisfied.

Imagine the following fragment of an explanatory chain, and let 'n' (with subscripts) stand for particular and general non-social facts, and let 's' (with subscripts) stand for particular and general social facts. Assume that no social facts reappear to the left of n_2.

$$n_2 \rightarrow s_3 \rightarrow n_1 \rightarrow s_2 \rightarrow s_1$$

I said before that the idea of an explanatory chain was a simplified abstraction, taken from explanatory trees, on which all universal, particular, and general facts required in an explanation were represented. In the fragment of the chain above, four universal facts would be required, if universal facts are required in the explanation of every general or particular fact. These are indeed laws, since universal facts are what laws are about:

(a) Whenever a fact like n_2, then a fact like s_3.
(b) Whenever a fact like s_3, then a fact like n_1.
(c) Whenever a fact like n_1, then a fact like s_2.
(d) Whenever a fact like s_2, then a fact like s_1.

I have stated (a)-(d) in the form of universally quantified laws. Since it is my intention to remain uncommitted on the question of whether a full explanation is deductive, it will make no difference to my argument if (a)-(d) were statistical in form, providing only inductive explanatory connections between the particular and general facts in the explanatory chain.

Either (a)-(d) have explanations or they do not. If they have no explanations, there will be irreducible, primitive social laws. If they have explanations, they will be either in terms of other social laws or in terms of non-social laws. Again, if the former, there seem to be irreducible social laws. Most forms of m.i. subscribe to the last possibility; social laws can be explained solely by means of non-social laws. On this view, social science can, in principle, be derived from psychology, plus the necessary bridge laws or correspondence rules having the form of biconditionals. Most forms of m.i. are committed to the explanation of laws like (a)-(d) by their reduction to, and hence their deduction from, non-social laws. (4), as stated, asserts just that, since the facts referred to in (4) cover universal, general, and particular facts.

There exist in the literature non-reductionist versions of

m.i. Since they leave social properties unreduced, and since they do not assert that the social is anomalous qua social, they must believe that there are some social laws, like (a)-(d), which cannot be explained solely in terms of non-social laws. They still might be able to give some sense to the idea of the explanatory priority of the non-social relative to the social, in spite of their need to accept unreduced social laws. They might accomplish this by restricting the scope of (4) – and of (4') which follows – to cover the cases only of particular and general facts, universal facts falling outside the scope of their claim. On such a modified, non-reductive view, this would still be true: for every social occurrence, and for every social feature or characteristic that something has, there will be a non-social occurrence or non-social feature of something which, together with social and non-social laws, explains it (this would have to be modified to cover the case of explanatory ancestors as well as explanations). Every such explanatory chain would be grounded in some non-social particular or general fact, although it would be a chain taken from a tree in which there were universal social facts not similarly grounded in non-social universal facts.

The reader may feel that this formulation of a non-reductive m.i. is insufficiently capable of capturing the vague idea of the explanatory priority of the non-social relative to the social to qualify as a bona fide example of m.i. The criticism of m.i. which I offer later, if it is sound, tells not only against the stronger version which covers universal as well as general and particular facts, but also against the restricted version limited only to the latter two kinds of facts. It is, therefore, not important to decide whether the restricted version is entitled to be called 'm.i.'. Whatever it is, my argument, if it is successful at all, succeeds against it.

Finally, I should like to make it clear that in (2), (3), (4) and later in (4') and (4"), the priority in question that one point in a chain has over another is *explanatory* priority, not necessarily temporal priority. If some fact is earlier in a chain than a second, it does not follow that the first fact occurred at a time prior to the second. It is a difficult question how explanatory and temporal priority are related, but whatever the answer, they are conceptually distinct. My claims concern only the former sort of priority, and not the latter.

Psychological versions of m.i.

Methodological individualists invariably say more than (4); they give some indication of what sorts of facts the non-social facts mentioned in (4) are. To be more precise, they have something to say only about a proper subset of explanatory chains, namely those which include at least one social fact. In terms of my earlier and ultimately inadequate formulation of m.i. (1), they have something to say only about the chains mentioned in the last four disjuncts, (1)(b)-(1)(e). (1)(a) covers, *inter alia*, cases of chemical explanations for explosions, meteorological explanations of the weather, and astronomic explanations for lunar eclipses. In what follows, when I speak of explanatory chains, I mean only that proper subset of them in which there is at least one social fact.

Different methodological individualists might have different views about what sorts of non-social facts meet the requirements of (4). Perhaps (e)-(g) are worth considering.

(e) psychological facts about the beliefs, desires, etc., of agents.
(f) psychological facts about agents and material facts about the world.
(g) (only) material facts about the world.

Although Mellor and Macdonald and Pettit write as if they subscribe to (e), it would be charitable to ascribe (f) to them. It might be that the psychological states of agents are insufficient by themselves to explain some objects of explanation, but become sufficient when conjoined with information about the material state of the world. The addition of the material states of the world is no concession from the point of view of m.i., and it could only serve to make the doctrine more plausible. If the addition is unnecessary, then adding it is harmless; if the addition is necessary, then we had better add it.

I refer to any version of m.i. which uses either (e) or (f) as 'a psychological version' of m.i. Now (g) does not yield a psychological version of m.i., but a version that we might call 'a materialist version'. I reserve, for discussion in an appendix to this chapter, yet another version of m.i., which follows from yet another restriction on what non-social facts will meet the requirements of (4).

A criticism of m.i. in any psychological version

Sometimes it is alleged that the fact that the psychological states of agents are themselves socially conditioned provides empirical refutation of m.i., at least in any psychological version. Is this so?

The literature is not at all clear about this, even the literature hostile to m.i. For example, Richard Miller says:

> As Watkins makes clear at several points in his essay, 'rock-bottom' does not mean 'final'. To adapt an example of Watkins', an individualist must require that an explanation of a population pattern in terms of tribal marriage customs rests on an individualistic explanation of those customs, perhaps in terms of beliefs and dispositions concerning incest. But the existence of the latter beliefs and dispositions might stand in need of further explanation. And the further explanation that initially comes to mind need not be wholly individualistic.[23]

Miller's commendable intention is to state m.i. in its most plausible form, before criticising it. But I doubt whether he has interpreted Watkins correctly, or whether the concession (if we delete 'that initially comes to mind' from Miller's final quoted sentence) is one that m.i. can consistently make.

First, let us address the question of interpretation. Miller cites two passages from Watkins to bear out this concession. In one of the passages that Miller cites, Watkins says that the tribesmen's dispositions to accept a certain system of rules 'could be explained individualistically in the sort of way that I can explain why my young children are already developing a typically English attitude towards police-men.'[24] There is no hint of a concession in this remark. In the other passage that Miller cites, Watkins asserts that an individual's decisions can be explained in terms of the individual's dispositions conjoined with a set of circumstances. In neither of the quoted passages, to which Miller refers, is there any indication that the explanation for agents' beliefs and dispositions might be given in non-individualistic terms.

Finally, Miller fails to mention this remark by Watkins:

> It has been objected that in making individual dispositions and beliefs and situations the terminus of an explanation in social science, methodological individualism implies that a person's psychological make-up is, so to speak, God-given, whereas it is in fact conditioned by, and ought to be explained in terms of, his social inheritance and environment. Now methodological individualism certainly does not prohibit attempts to explain the formation of psychological characteristics; it only requires that such explanations should in turn be *individualistic*.[25]

Watkins, then, seems firmly to reject non-individualistic explanation of agents' psychological states. Miller's concession on the explanation of psychological states which he wishes to attribute to Watkins is not a concession that Watkins accepts.

Of more interest than the point about the correct interpretation of what Watkins said is the question of consistency: could Watkins, or any methodological individualist holding the doctrine in a psychological version, have consistently made the concession that Miller urges?

At one level, methodological individualists can certainly admit that we sometimes correctly offer social or sociological explanations for the psychological states in which agents find themselves. A version of m.i. that claimed that this was always a mistake would surely be too implausible to warrant further consideration. Sometimes we believe such things as that a certain individual thinks something because of his social circumstances and position. Although this sort of explanation is subject to great misuse, especially because of its indiscriminate employment, no one believes that these sorts of explanations can *never* be right.

But if remarks like this about the social conditioning of psychological states are unproblematically sometimes correct, exactly what is it that the methodological individualist asserts that his opponent would deny? We can see the answer to this if we use (f) to specify the non-social facts we are now chasing, and reformulate (4) with this in mind:

(4') For every explanatory chain which includes at least one social fact, there is some point in the chain at which the facts are only psychological (and material) facts, and such that *either* there are no facts prior to that point at all, *or*, if there are, no facts prior to that point are social facts.

(4') offers a choice to the methodological individualist. We can simplify matters by dismissing the first of the two choices. If he were a contra-causal libertarian, he might hold that the individual choices and decisions which explain social facts had themselves no further explanation. Of course, neither Watkins nor any other methodological individualist of whom I am aware would grasp at such a straw. Unless he pursues this unpromising line of thought, he will be committed to believing that these psychological facts about agents have explanations, and explanatory ancestors, none of which are or include any social facts. Hereafter, I assume that the methodological individualist is so committed.

Many psychological facts can have social explanations, or social facts as explanatory ancestors, according to (4'). What (4') says is that in every explanatory chain which includes a social fact, there must be some psychological facts which neither are explained by any social facts nor have any social facts as explanatory ancestors. As Watkins expressed this, m.i., in a psychological version, must insist that the explanations of the formation of psychological characteristics 'should in turn be individualistic'. To deny that these chains of explanations become individualistic at *some* psychological point (but perhaps not at the specific point Watkins

165

mentions), and remain so no matter how far back in the chain one goes, would be to make a concession inconsistent with m.i. in a psychological version.

I find (4') utterly implausible (this is, of course, an observation, not an argument). Notice just how strong (4') is. It makes a claim about *every* explanatory chain which includes *any* social fact, and says that at some point on the chain, there will be *only* psychological (and material) facts, such that *none* of them has a social explanation or any social explanatory ancestor. Although I believe that (4') is false, I could certainly accept that *some* psychological characteristics, dispositions, etc., may be innate, or anyway the explanation of whose acquisition does not require any social facts. But (4') is very much stronger than just that. It does not just need the truth, if indeed it is one, that *some* psychological characteristics are innate, or anyway are such that their explanations and explanatory ancestors include no social facts. Rather, it needs the claim that at some point in every explanatory chain with a social fact there are only psychological (and material) facts, none of whose explanations or explanatory ancestors includes social facts, and this is a very strong claim indeed.

The argument I offer for the falsity of (4') relies on the idea of rationally held true belief, and the conditions which make this sort of belief possible. Suppose that a person rationally holds some true belief, for instance the particular belief that an object o is P. What must be the case for the person to rationally hold such a true belief? In the standard case (I want to avoid complications that arise in deviant causal chain cases and in Gettier-style examples), if a person p rationally holds the true belief that o is P, then part of the explanation of why he holds this belief is that o is P. Some readers will be attracted by expressing this in causal terms, but this commitment is unnecessary here. Expressing it in terms of explanation allows us to capture uncontroversially more than the same claim would permit only controversially if at all if expressed in causal terms. For example, if a person rationally holds the true belief that $2 + 2 = 4$, part of the explanation of why he believes this is that $2 + 2 = 4$. This may be uncapturable in causal terms, but it is certainly capturable in terms of explanation of true, rational belief.

Now, the central claim of m.i. in a psychological version is that we can explain social facts by means of agents' beliefs and other psychological states. Other states might be included – attitudes like loyalty for instance – but I shall assume hereafter that some cognitive states, like belief, must be included in the psychological states which are meant to be the explanans-entities or explanatory ancestors for social facts. Statements of m.i. in a psychological version have always included beliefs among the psychological states, as inspection of the quotations from Mellor, Watkins, and Macdonald and Pettit that I have used so far in this chapter will bear out.

I have made much of the fact that the methodological individualist is entitled to free access to social properties (and to social objects too) in giving content to those cognitive states. I am unaware of a single contemporary methodological individualist who does not employ social properties or objects in giving content to those psychological states. This is not a criticism of m.i.; it is merely to state m.i. in an initially plausible form. That is to say, what contemporary methodological individualists propose is that we explain social facts by means, *inter alia*, of agents' beliefs about social facts. Mellor brings out this assumption quite explicitly:

> Reducing social facts to people's beliefs about social facts might seem beer too small and easy to be worth brewing. Social concepts have after all to be used to identify the very psychological states. . . . That they then redeliver the social facts believed in, may seem neither surprising nor significant.[26]

Mellor goes on to defend the thesis that social facts can be explained by (indeed he thinks they can be reduced to) people's beliefs about social facts, defending the explanation from the charge of insignificance.

We are examining a thesis about explanation, not specifically about reduction. My criticism of the idea that one can explain social facts by means, *inter alia*, of people's beliefs about social facts is *not* that social facts must be used in the identification of the contents of the belief states. It is, rather, that in so far as this is done, methodological individualism reverses the correct order of explanation. If social agents rationally hold true beliefs about social facts, then part of the explanation of why they are in those cognitive states is that those social facts do obtain. In the case of rationally held true belief, we don't explain the social facts by means of agents' beliefs about social facts; we explain the beliefs about social facts in part by the social facts. For example, if I rationally hold the true belief that some societies are matrilineal, or that La Guardia was mayor of New York, part of the reason for my having the beliefs, which partly explains why I have them, is that some societies are matrilineal, and that La Guardia was mayor of New York.

I have already said that I will assume that the methodological individualist will hold: that the psychological states required by (4′) will have explanations; that cognitive states like belief will be included among them; and that the content of these cognitive states will be describable only by using descriptions of social properties or social objects or both. Subject to these three assumptions, (4′) commits the methodological individualist to:

(5) The beliefs required by (4′) are either untrue, or not rationally held.

Since such cognitive states (or the fact that agents are in such cognitive states) is supposed to explain the social facts the beliefs are about, the beliefs of the agents could hardly be untrue. So, the methodological individualist will have to believe that they are not rationally held (in spite of being true). Why should we accept that agents ever (no matter how far back we are prepared to go in the evolutionary story) non-rationally held such beliefs about social facts?

There are some parallels between this consequence of m.i. and a consequence of phenomenalism. We normally believe that we can explain why agents are in certain non-cognitive sensory states by reference to physical objects. For example, part of the explanation of why percipients sense something round (in the normal, veridical case) is the presence of a round object. If phenomenalism is true, there is a sense in which this explanation is, from a philosophical point of view, illusory (although the phenomenalist might license our continuing to speak in such ways in ordinary discourse). If objects are just sets of actual and possible sensory experiences, then one cannot really (from a philosophical point of view) explain why people sense something round by reference to the presence of round objects. If nothing can explain itself, then nothing can explain a part of itself either. That is, one cannot explain the sensing of something round by reference to a set of actual and possible sensory experiences, to which the explanandum sensory experience belongs.

Consider, then, these two 'ordinary' assertions:

(6) In normal cases, part of the explanation of why persons rationally hold the true belief that they are sensing something round is the fact that there is something round nearby.

(7) In normal cases, part of the explanation of why persons rationally hold the true belief that some societies are matrilineal is the fact that some societies are matrilineal.

Just as phenomenalism makes (6), from a philosophical point of view, an illusion, so too m.i. makes it incomprehensible how (7), from a philosophical point of view, could still be true.

I do not expect that Mellor, or any methodological individualist, will find my argument irresistible. No doubt a reply will be that all of this can be rendered anodyne from a methodological individualist's point of view by further reducing the social fact that some societies are matrilineal to some psychological facts, and hence preserving the methodological individualist's ability to retain assertions like (7). My point is that all of this work has simply been left undone by the claim we are considering. If the methodological individualist has some further move he can make which will show that his point of view is consistent with the requirement that rationally held true beliefs about social facts are partly explained by social facts, and not vice versa, he has yet to make that move. The phenomenalist response to (6) is that the fact that people have whatever sensory experience they do have is just a brute, inexplicable fact about them. We have already ruled out, as implausible, the idea that being in such cognitive states about social facts are such brute, inexplicable facts about persons. If we are barred from letting social facts play their accustomed part in the explanatory story for these cognitive states, it is not easy to see what else could play this role.

If sociology or social science could be fully explained by psychology, then the former could be no more 'objective' than is morality on a non-cognitivist interpretation. On such a non-cognitivist interpretation of morality, from the point of view of rationality, our highest-level moral beliefs are to be explained by our ultimate commitments, not by any appreciation of the facts about moral reality. The non-cognitivist about morality may well allow explanations of why we make just the sorts of ultimate commitments that we do make, the point being that since there are no explanations in terms of the moral facts of the matter, such explanation does not confer rationality on these ultimate commitments.

Methodological individualism in a psychological version asks us to accept something surprisingly similar about social science. If our beliefs about society, at least the highest-level ones, cannot be explained in terms of the social facts of the matter, then whatever does explain them will not be such as to confer rationality on them. I do not deny that there is a closer connection, in some sense, between what we believe about society and what the social facts are than there is between what we believe about the shape of objects and the shape that physical objects have. But the connection is simply not as close as m.i. requires.

My argument, if sound, does not show that sociology cannot be derived from psychology (although I hope my arguments in chapters 1 and 3 show that it cannot). What my argument here shows is that psychology cannot explain sociology. There are many good arguments in the literature that show that derivability of an explanandum from an explanans that meets all of Hempel's formal and material conditions is *insufficient* for explanation.[27] Even if sociology were deductively derivable from psychology, whatever more is required for explanation is surely missing in just this case.

I conclude that (4') is in fact false. I have been careful throughout to say only that (4') formulates a psychological version of m.i., and that I have offered some considerations which argue for its falsity. There can be non-psychological versions of m.i., obtainable for example by reading (4) in combination with (g). I call such a version 'methodological materialism':

(4'')   For every explanatory chain which includes at least one social fact, there is some point in the chain at which the facts are only material facts, and such that *either* there are no facts prior to that point at all, *or*, if there are, then no facts prior to that point are social facts.[28]

Below is a fragment of an explanatory chain that meets the requirements of (4''). I let 'm' and 'p' (with subscripts) stand for material and psychological facts respectively. I assume that no social fact reappears at any point in the chain (or indeed in the tree) to the left of m_1. As before, 's' (with subscripts) stands for social facts.

$$m_1 \rightarrow s_3 \rightarrow p_2 \rightarrow p_1 \rightarrow s_2 \rightarrow s_1$$

Methodological materialism makes material, rather than psychological, facts prior in explanatory prowess to social facts. In the chain above, the contrast in explanatory power is between material and social facts, not between psychological and social facts.

The general idea of m.i., in any version, is that there is some asymmetry in explanatory power between social facts and some other kind of facts, that the latter can explain the former in a way in which the former cannot explain the latter. My criticism of m.i. did not focus on this general idea, but rather on the specific idea that it was psychological facts which could play this asymmetric explanatory role *vis-à-vis* social facts. On reflection, I think psychology proves a particularly implausible place to look for a large number of facts, none of whose explanans-entities or explanatory ancestors are social facts. Sciences of the material – chemistry, physics – are far more likely places to find facts which meet this requirement.

I am not asking the reader to take seriously the idea that methodological materialism is true. It is not surprising, I think, that no modern version of m.i. has ever been cast in this form. The general idea of explanatory asymmetry itself has two parts. First, we need facts of one kind which can explain facts of another kind. Second, facts of the first kind must have no facts of the second kind among their explanans-entities or explanatory ancestors (this being required to give sense to the idea of explanatory asymmetry). It is not implausible that chemical or physical facts can fulfil the second requirement, unlike psychology which cannot. But it is most implausible to think that chemical or physical facts can fulfil the first part of the requirement, unlike psychology, where the thought is at least not initially implausible. The chances of m.i. being true, whether in a psychological or non-psychological version, seem then to be very slim indeed.

First appendix
to Chapter 4

One of the most influential contemporary philosophers who has espoused a doctrine called 'methodological individualism' is Karl Popper. As I will make clear, (4') cannot be attributed to him. The purpose of this appendix is to formulate what I take to be Popper's methodological individualism. I doubt whether the formulation I produce in this appendix adequately captures everything Popper has ever said about methodological individualism. It certainly captures, though, one of his leading ideas.

I noted in chapter 4 Popper's rejection of psychologism. Although psychologism has historically been espoused as a doctrine about reduction, the reduction of sociology to psychology, if we expressed the same idea in terms of explanation rather than reduction, the resulting doctrine would be very close indeed to (4'). If this is, then, what Popper *rejects*, one might wonder what it could possibly mean when it is said that he supports m.i.

Here is a typical statement by Popper of what he means by 'm.i.':

> All social phenomena . . . should always be understood as resulting from the desires, actions, attitudes, etc. of human individuals, and we should never be satisfied by an explanation in terms of so-called 'collectives' (states, nations, races).[1]

Neither desires nor attitudes take us beyond what is available to the supporter of psychologism. But actions do, or might. The point is that Popper appears to place no restrictions on the ways in which we can refer to actions, and hence no restrictions on the actions which we are entitled to use in our explanations. As part of an ultimately acceptable explanans-entity, I may include facts about the social actions of individuals. I might include such facts as the fact that : so-and-so voted, he cashed a cheque, he went to a bank, he followed a rule, he exchanged something, and so on. Popper does not intend that we should exclude all social facts from our ultimately acceptable explanantia.

This is confirmed in the second part of the quote, in which he specifies the proper subset of social facts that are to be excluded from ultimately acceptable explanantia: those social facts which are about states, nations, or races. In other words, assuming that states, nations, and races are meant to be *examples* rather than a definitive list of what is to be excluded, what Popper excludes from ultimately acceptable explanantia are only social facts about social entitites, and no other kinds of social facts. Popper intends a different explanatory asymmetry than the one formulated by (4'). (4') states an explanatory priority of non-social over social facts generally. Popper argues for an explanatory priority of facts not about social entities (this includes both non-social facts and social facts not about social entities) over facts about social entities.

That this is what Popper intends is further borne out by his discussion of situational logic. What is meant to distinguish Popper from the supporters of psychologism is his insistence that the decisions, desires, attitudes, and so on of agents can themselves only be understood in terms of the logic of the situation in which agents find themselves. Popper makes quite clear both by what he says about the logic of the situation and the examples of it he gives that the relevant logic is the logic of a *social* situation: 'This social situation is hardly reducible to motives and the general laws of "human nature".'[2] Two of his examples are these: that an individual's craving for power can only be understood in the context of the modern family, and that the knowledge economic agents have can only be understood 'in terms of the *social* situation – the market situation'.[3] In volume I of *The Open Society and Its Enemies*, Popper praises a discussion of tyranny by Plato as being a particularly insightful treatment of situational logic,[4] so it is clear that he is thinking of tyranny as constituting an admissible fact to be cited in the explanation of agents' psychological states.

Popper's m.i. permits social facts about tyranny, the market, and the modern family as ultimately acceptable explanans-entities, as long as these facts can be understood as facts that social properties are true of individuals, and not facts about social entities like races, classes, nations, and states. (Actually, races are not social at all, but purportedly biological. But we let this pass.)

I do not feel confident that, on the basis of the evidence of the texts, I can decide whether Watkins subscribes to (4') or to Popper's version of m.i. On the one hand, he explicitly follows Popper in rejecting psychologism, which is close to, if not identical with, (4'). On the other hand, his remarks embody an ambiguity over just this issue. In the quote from Watkins on which we based our initial formulation of m.i., Watkins required that we deduce an account of large-scale social phenomena from 'statements about the dispositions, beliefs, (physical) resources, and interrelations of individuals'. He does not say whether the interrelations he has in mind are material and psychological interrelations only, or whether they include social interrelations. If the former, we can ascribe (4') to him; if the latter, he would seem to subscribe to Popper's m.i. In an earlier formulation of m.i., Watkins stressed that the explanation of social phenomena should be deduced from 'principles governing the behaviour of individuals . . . and descriptions of their situations'.[5] This embodies the same ambiguity as the first formulation I quoted. Are we restricted to their physical and psychological situation in offering such explanations, or are we permitted to include facts about their social situations? As far as I know, everything Watkins says (other than his explicit rejection of psychologism) is consistent with ascribing (4') to him and with ascribing Popper's m.i. to him. To that extent, Watkins formulation of m.i. is simply vague. In the body of chapter 4, I construed Watkins as subscribing to (4'). This construal must be placed in some doubt.

Is Popper's m.i. more plausible than (4')? It is more plausible, in the sense that it places fewer restrictions on ultimately acceptable explanantia. Only facts about social entities are excluded, rather than all social facts whatever.

But it seems subject to the same argument that I used against (4'). Sometimes we believe things about social entities – races, classes, nations, institutions – as well as believe that social properties are true of individuals. For example, we may believe that France is a charter member of the United Nations. In so far as we rationally believe this and the belief is true, part of the explanation of why we believe this must be that France is a charter member of the United Nations. Here too, the explanatory story gives every appearance of going in the opposite direction from that required by Popper's m.i. Facts about social entities partly explain why individuals hold true, rational beliefs about social entities. Perhaps the theory can be made consistent with this, but, as it stands, the theory gives no hint of how this consistency might be achieved.

Second appendix
to Chapter 4

In *Judging Justice*, Philip Pettit offers some considerations which are meant to tell against the idea that we can sometimes explain why persons hold beliefs about social facts by citing social facts:[1]

> If an object is perceptually salient, in the sense that consistently with the perceptual cues and circumstances it is inevitable that the percipient identify it in some sense, then we may reasonably say that a causal interaction between that object and the percipient accounts for the attitude held in respect of it to which the perception gives rise. . . . The idea proposed by the institutionalist is that a similar interaction between people and institutions must be postulated to explain the formation of certain attitudes which the people hold in respect of the institutions.

Pettit concludes that the idea is 'unpersuasive', on the grounds that: 'Institutions are not perceptually salient objects.' 'The perceptual interaction . . . that lies at the base of certain attitudes which agents form in respect of institutions is not interaction with the institutions themselves but with those items which they take as evidential tokens of the institutions.'

As it stands, Pettit's argument is certainly fallacious. Its opening line asserts that perceptual salience of an object is, *ceteris paribus*, a *sufficient* condition for saying that a causal interaction between object and percipient can explain the percipient's belief or attitudes about the object. But then Pettit argues that institutions are not the right sort of objects for saying that a causal interaction between them and percipients explains percipients' beliefs and attitudes about them, on the grounds of the perceptual non-salience of institutions. That is, Pettit assumes without argument and apparently without even noticing the switch that an object's perceptual salience is a *necessary* condition for saying that a causal interaction between object and percipient can (partly) explain the percipient's beliefs and attitudes about the object. It is only by assuming that this is a necessary condition that Pettit can dismiss institutions in the way he does.

Had he correctly formulated the premiss his argument needs, he might the more readily have detected its implausibility. Consider the case of unobservable entities in natural science: subatomic particles, waves, force fields, and black holes. None of these things is perceptually salient. However, if a scientist rationally holds a true belief about a subatomic particle, part of the explanation of why he believes this is that the subatomic particles are indeed like that. The fact that the particle is like that will not be the immediate explanation; the explanatory chain from the movement of the particles to the scientist's belief about the movement of the particles will pass through facts about observable events like paths in Wilson cloud chambers and lines on spectroscopes. There is no requirement that objects not perceptually salient be the immediate (part) explanation of beliefs about non-perceptually salient objects. They can be (part of) the mediate or remote explanation. In such cases, the explanatory chains will include the inferential activity of agents as well as their perceptions. For example, to return to a social case, a fuller aetiology of the belief that La Guardia was mayor of New York might look like this:

L.G. was mayor of New York → L.G. wore the keys of the City on some occasion → N.N. observed that L.G. wore the keys → N.N. inferred that L.G. was mayor → N.N. believed that L.G. was mayor.

There are two points on which my and Pettit's arguments do not quite join. First, Pettit limits his disqualification from playing an explanatory role to institutions, but my argument covers all cases of social facts. Pettit's notion of perceptual salience is intended as a replacement for the older idea of observability: something is perceptually salient if and only if 'consistently with the perceptual cues and circumstances it is inevitable that the percipient identify it in some sense'. Perceptual salience inherits all the unclarities and difficulties that the old term had. If there is a problem about the observability of institutions, there ought to be a problem about the observability of someone's being a mayor. That La Guardia is a mayor is no more or less observable than a social group is. If I can observe that he is a mayor by observing what he is wearing (and identifying it as what mayors wear), then I can observe a social group by observing a member (and identifying him as a member of the group). So if there is a problem about observability, it should be expressed as a difficulty with social facts generally, and not just as a difficulty with institutions. Second, Pettit speaks in terms of *causal interactions*; I speak in terms of *explanation* of beliefs, for reasons I have already mentioned. As they have throughout this chapter, the arrows in the diagrams of explanatory chains stand for the explanation relation, not the causal relation.

Notes

Chapter 1

1　J.W.N. Watkins, 'Historical explanation in the social sciences', *British Journal for the Philosophy of Science*, vol. 8, 1957, reprinted in John O'Neill (ed.), *Modes of Individualism and Collectivism*, London, Heinemann, 1973, pp. 166-78. Quote from fn., p. 169.

2　A. Quinton, 'Social objects', *Proceedings of the Aristotelian Society*, vol. 76, 1975-6, p. 3.

3　M. Mandelbaum, 'Societal facts', *The British Journal of Sociology*, vol. 6, 1955, reprinted in J. O'Neill (ed.), *op. cit.*, pp. 221-34. Quote from p. 227.

4　D.M. Armstrong, *Perception and the Physical World*, London, Routledge & Kegan Paul, 1963, pp. 47-52.

5　A standard account of theory reduction can be found in E. Nagel, *The Structure of Science*, New York, Harcourt, Brace & World, 1961, pp. 336-97. The example of mirror images is mentioned by D.H. Mellor, 'The reduction of society', *Philosophy*, no. 57, 1982, pp. 51-75, on pp. 54-5, but in order to make a point directly opposite to the one I make.

6　The importance of this distinction for the debate in the philosophy of social science about individualism and holism was suggested to me by S. Lukes, 'Methodological individualism reconsidered', *The British Journal of Sociology*, vol. 19, 1968, pp. 119-29; reprinted in A. Ryan (ed.), *The Philosophy of Social Explanation*, Oxford University Press, 1973, pp. 119-29.

7　W.V.O. Quine, *Word and Object*, Cambridge, Mass., MIT Press, 1960, p. 242.

8　Cf. W. Lycan and G. Pappas, 'What is eliminative materialism?', *Australasian Journal of Philosophy*, vol. 50, 1972, no. 2, pp. 149-59.

9　A. Quinton, *op. cit.*, pp. 8-9. I quote Quinton's remarks only as suggestive of an argument for the conclusion that belief in the existence of social substances could have no possible empirical warrant. Quinton himself does not use these remarks to argue to such a conclusion.

10　A. Quinton, *op. cit.*, p. 9; J.W.N. Watkins, 'Methodological individualism: a reply', *Philosophy of Science*, vol. 21, 1954, no. 2; reprinted in J. O'Neill (ed.), *op. cit.*, pp. 179-84. Quote from p. 183.

11　B. Russell, *Human Knowledge: Its Scope and Limits*, London, Allen &

Unwin, 1948, p. 296.

12 Michael Lessnoff, *The Structure of Social Science*, London, Allen & Unwin, 1974, p. 79.

13 H.L.A. Hart, *The Concept of Law*, Oxford University Press, 1961, pp. 92-107.

14 D. Papineau, *For Science in the Social Sciences*, London, Macmillan, 1979, p. 108.

15 *Ibid.*

16 Philip Pettit, *Judging Justice*, London, Routledge & Kegan Paul, 1980, pp. 61-2. He does not make the remark in the context of attempting a reductive identification. Indeed, he accepts that entity holism is true, and argues only for methodological individualism, although his comparison of social entities with sets suggests that he has not grasped the difference between social and abstract objects.
Thus, I do not miss Pettit's point, as he asserts in his 'In defence of "A new methodological individualism": Reply to J.E. Tiles', *Ratio*, vol. 26, 1984, no. 1, p. 85, fn. 8. I do not take my two arguments in this chapter as directed against Pettit's position at all, but only against someone arguing 'against the reality . . . of s-items' rather than their 'token-explanatory autonomy'.

17 Arthur Pap, 'Indubitable existential statements', *Mind*, vol. 55, 1946, pp. 234-46.

18 Peter Unger, *Ignorance: A Case for Scepticism*, Oxford University Press, 1975, pp. 70-4.

19 Crispin Wright, *Frege's Conception of Numbers As Objects*, Aberdeen University Press, 1983, pp. 99-100.

20 *Ibid.*, pp. 101-3.

21 D.H. Mellor, *op. cit.*, p. 72.

22 D.M. Armstrong, *op. cit.*, pp. 105-22. The idea is that an object o's appearing red to person p is just p's disposition to believe that o is red.

23 G. Currie, 'Individualism and global supervenience' *British Journal for the Philosophy of Science*, forthcoming.

Chapter 2

1 Anthony Quinton, 'Social objects', *Proceedings of the Aristotelian Society*, vol. 76, 1975-6, pp. 1-27. Quote from p. 5.

2 Graham Macdonald and Philip Pettit, *Semantics and Social Science*, London, Routledge & Kegan Paul, 1981, p. 108.

3 Arthur Danto, 'Methodological individualism and methodological socialism', *Filosofia*. vol. 4, 1962. Reprinted in John O'Neill (ed.), *Modes of Individualism and Collectivism*, London, Heinemann, 1973, pp. 312-37. Quote from p. 313.

4 Paul Oppenheim and Hilary Putnam, 'Unity of science as a working hypothesis', in H. Feigl, G. Maxwell, and M. Scriven (eds), *Minnesota Studies in the Philosophy of Science*, vol. 2, Minneapolis, University of Minesota Press, 1958, pp. 3-36.

5   Cf. David and Stephanie Lewis, 'Holes', *Australasian Journal of Philosophy*, vol. 48, 1970, pp. 206-12.
6   Nicholas Rescher, 'Axioms for the part relation', *Philosophical Studies*, vol. 6, 1955, pp. 8-11. See (3), p. 10 in that article.
7   Alvin Plantinga, 'On mereological essentialism', *Review of Metaphysics*, vol. 28, 1974-5, pp. 468-76, and followed by a rejoinder by Chisholm.
8   Roderick Chisholm, 'Parts as essential to their wholes', *Review of Metaphysics*, vol. 26, 1972-3, pp. 581-603.
9   Roderick Chisholm, *Person and Object*, London, Allen & Unwin, 1976, Appendix, pp. 145-58.
10 Roderick Chisholm, 'Parts as essential to their wholes', p. 583.
11 Tyler Burge, 'A theory of aggregates', *Nous*, vol. 11, 1977, pp. 97-117. A similar distinction is made by David Wiggins in 'On being in the same place at the same time', *Philosophical Review*, vol. 77, 1968, pp. 90-5.
12 Nicholas Rescher, *op. cit.* See (4), p. 10 in his article.
13 *Ibid.*, (2), p. 10.
14 David Armstrong, *Universals and Scientific Realism: Nominalism and Realism*, vol. 1, Cambridge University Press, 1978, p. 121.
15 David Wiggins, *op. cit.*, p. 94.
16 A well-known statement of this point of view is by P.F. Strawson, *Individuals*, London, Methuen, 1959, pp. 38-58.
17 The importance for Gestalt psychology of the part-whole relation, and the conditions governing that relation as it is used by Gestalt psychology, has been discussed by (among others) Nicholas Rescher and Paul Oppenheim, 'Logical analysis of Gestalt concepts', *The British Journal for the Philosophy of Science*, vol. 6, 1955, pp.89-106.
18 David Wiggins, *op. cit.*, p. 93.
19 David Wiggins, *Sameness and Substance*, Oxford, Basil Blackwell, 1980, p. 7.
20 P.F. Strawson, *op. cit.*, p. 168.

Chapter 3

1   D.M. Armstrong, *A Theory of Universals: Universals and Scientific Realism*, vol. 3, Cambridge University Press, 1980, pp. 19-23.
2   It is true, though, that I do accept it as a distinct category. I say something in defence of distinguishing it from logical necessity in my 'Marx, necessity, and science', in G.H.R. Parkinson (ed.), *Marx and Marxisms*, Cambridge University Press, 1982, especially pp. 46-9.
3   Hilary Putnam, 'The mental life of some machines', reprinted in Hilary Putnam, *Mind, Language, and Reality: Philosophical Papers*, vol. 2; Colin McGinn, 'Mental states, natural kinds, and psychophysical laws', *The Aristotelian Society suppl. vol. 52*, 1978, pp. 195-220; Jaegwon Kim, 'Supervenience and nomological incommensurables', *American Philosophical Quarterly*, vol. 15, 1979, pp. 149-56.
4   Colin McGinn, *op. cit.*, p. 204.
5   *Ibid.*, p. 205.

6 Hilary Putnam, *op. cit.*, p. 418.

7 I owe thanks to Dr R.M. Sainsbury and Professor Neil Tennant, both of whom helped me to see this point more clearly.

8 D.M. Armstrong, *op. cit.*, p. 20.

9 Hilary Putnam, 'Philosophy and our mental life', reprinted in Hilary Putnam, *Mind, Language, and Reality: Philosophical Papers, vol. 2*, Cambridge University Press, 1980, pp. 291-303. All succeeding references to p. 299.

10 Alan Garfinkel, *Forms of Explanation: Rethinking the Questions in Social Theory*, New Haven, Yale University Press, 1981, p. 85.

11 A. Quinton, 'Social objects', *Proceedings of the Aristotelian Society*, vol. 76, 1975-6, pp. 2-3.

12 D.S. Shwayder, *The Stratification of Behaviour*, London, Routledge & Kegan Paul, 1965, pp. 250-2. A similar account is offered by David Lewis, in *Convention: A Philosophical Study*, Cambridge, Mass., Harvard University Press, 1977. See especially chapters 1-3.

13 D.S. Shwayder, *op. cit.*, pp. 252-63.

14 I tried to say something about this distinction in my 'Warnock on rules', *Philosophical Quarterly*, vol. 22, 1972, no. 89, pp. 349-54.

15 For the uninitiated, see Karl Marx, *Capital*, vol. I, Moscow, Progress Publishers, 1965, part I, section 4, pp. 71-83 ('The fetishism of commodities and the secret thereof').

16 'I begin by distinguishing between act-types and act-tokens. An act-type is simply an act-property. . . . To perform the act, then, is to exemplify a property.' Alvin Goldman, *A Theory of Human Action*, Princeton University Press, 1970, pp.10-11.

17 But why suppose that there *are* properties at all? Can't we simply refuse to quantify over properties? This will hardly do in the context of this discussion, since we are discussing whether one property is identical with another. The whole discussion is predicated on the assumption that it makes perfectly good sense to speak of the existence of properties. But can't we suppose that, although there are properties, they are only sets (or whatever else one's favourite reductive candidate might be)? Since any such reduction will have to provide parsing of talk about properties and their identities, the contents of this paper will apply, *mutatis mutandis*, to whatever reduces properties and the identities of these.

Suppose someone believes that something is a round square, or that some set is a member of the set of all sets that are not members of themselves. Is there, in these cases, a property such that I believe that something has it? I would be willing to qualify my claim so that it covers only those cases in which 'x is P' is not inconsistent or contradictory, although whether such a qualification is necessary is controversial. I am, though, committed to there being such a property even when, as a matter of contingent fact, the property is uninstantiated, so my claim is inconsistent with the view that a property exists only if at least one thing has that property.

18 If 'q' is an analysis of 'p' and if 'r' is an analysis of 'q', then 'r' is a

remote analysis of 'p'.

19 J.W.N. Watkins, 'Ideal types and historical explanation', reprinted in John O'Neill (ed.), *Modes of Individualism and Collectivism*, London, Heinemann, 1973, p. 159.

Appendix to Chapter 3

1 Steven Lukes, 'Methodological individualism reconsidered', reprinted in Alan Ryan (ed.), *The Philosophy of Social Explanation*, Oxford University Press, 1973, pp. 119-29. All quotations from pp. 125-6.

Chapter 4

1 Peter Achinstein, 'The object of explanation', in Stephan Korner (ed.), *Explanation*, Oxford, Basil Blackwell, 1975, pp. 1-45.

2 Donald Davidson, Causal relations', reprinted in Ernest Sosa (ed.), *Causation and Conditionals*, Oxford University Press, 1975, p. 93.

3 Carl Hempel, *Aspects of Scientific Explanation*, New York, Free Press, 1970, p. 247.

4 *Ibid.*, p. 233.

5 See, for example, the symposium between J.L. Austin and Peter Strawson, 'Truth', *Proceedings of the Aristotelian Society*, suppl. vol. 24, 1950. Also D.J. O'Connor, *The Correspondence Theory of Truth*, London, Hutchinson, 1975, *passim*.

6 Alan Garfinkel, *Forms of Explanation: Rethinking the Questions in Social Theory*, New Haven, Yale University Press, 1981, chapter 1.

7 It seems to me that Fred Dretske's 'Contrastive statements' (*Philosophical Review*, vol. 82, 1973, pp. 411-37) is fundamentally in error in its neglect of this point. Suppose Alex is unemployed and needs some money. Clyde lends Alex $300. Suppose I ask you why Clyde lent Alex $300, and you tell me that it is because Alex needed money, Clyde only loans and never gives, there was no one else around in a position to help Alex, and Clyde, knowing this, felt obliged. Dretske concludes that 'there is nothing odd or incorrect in saying that' (p. 417) you have explained to me why Clyde lent Alex $300. This seems patently 'incorrect', although – exceptional circumstances apart – only a pedant would point out the incorrectness. You have explained to me why Clyde lent Alex some money, but not explained why he lent him $300.

8 Carl Hempel, *op. cit.*, pp. 333-425, and *passim*.

9 See for example the following: Bas Van Fraassen, *The Scientific Image*, Oxford University Press, 1980, pp. 104-6 (from which the quotation in the text derives); R.C. Jeffrey, 'Statistical explanation vs statistical inference', and W.C. Salmon, 'Statistical explanation', both in W.C. Salmon *et al.* (eds), *Statistical Explanation and Statistical Relevance*, University of Pittsburgh Press, 1971, pp. 19-28 and pp. 29-87 respectively.

10 D.H. Mellor, 'Probable explanation', *Australasian Journal of Philosophy*, vol. 54, 1976, no. 3, pp. 231-41.

11 Michael Scriven, 'Truisms as the grounds for historical explanations', reprinted in P. Gardiner (ed.), *Theories of History*, New York, Free Press, 1959, pp. 443-75. Quote from p. 467.

12 William Dray, 'Historical explanation of actions reconsidered', reprinted in P. Gardiner (ed.), *The Philosophy of History*, Oxford University Press, 1978, pp. 66-89. Reference to p. 78.

13 Carl Hempel, *op. cit.*, pp. 390-1.

14 The explanation that Hempel contrasts with the explanation of a particular event is an explanation of an actual, empirical series of events by a statistical law, and it is this that he assumes is admitted by all parties to the dispute to be an inductive explanation. Whatever it is, it should not be confused with the sort of deductive explanation described by May Brodbeck in 'Explanation, prediction, and "Imperfect Knowledge" ', in *Minnesota Studies* 3, pp. 231-72: 'If an unbiased coin is tossed a large number of times, then the frequency with which heads will turn up is 50%. This says something about the class of all tosses of a coin. . .' (p. 248). The law that the flipping of a fair coin yields heads with the probability of $\frac{1}{2}$ can only deductively entail something about the class of *all* tosses of a coin (at least on one theory of probability), but it will only inductively support a conclusion about any actual series of a specific number of tossings.

15 William Dray, *op. cit.*, p. 87.

16 See for example the remarks by Robert Nozick, *Philosophical Explanations*, Oxford University Press, 1981, pp. 116-17, and fn. 3 on p. 668.

17 Graham Macdonald and Philip Pettit, *Semantics and Social Science*, London, Routledge & Kegan Paul, 1981, p. 125.

18 J.W.N. Watkins, 'Historical explanation in the social sciences', reprinted in J. O'Neill (ed.), *Modes of Individualism and Collectivism*, London, Heinemann, 1973, p. 168.

19 D.H. Mellor, 'The reduction of society', *Philosophy*, vol. 57, 1982, pp. 51-75.

20 *Ibid.*, p. 72.

21 K.R. Popper, *The Open Society and Its Enemies*, vol. 2, London, Routledge & Kegan Paul, 1969, chapter 14. See p. 90 for his definition of 'psychologism'.

22 *Ibid.*, pp. 92-3.

23 Richard Miller, 'Methodological individualism and social explanation', *Philosophy of Science*, vol. 45, 1978, pp. 387-414. Quote from pp. 389-90.

24 J.W.N. Watkins, *op. cit.*, p. 173, fn. 6.

25 *Ibid.*, pp. 171-2.

26 D.H. Mellor, *op. cit.*, p. 72.

27 My favourite example is from A. Lyon, 'The relevance of Wisdom's work for the philosophy of science', in R. Bambrough (ed.), *Wisdom: Twelve Essays*, Oxford, Basil Blackwell, 1974, p. 247. The example is this: (1) All metals conduct electricity, and (2) Whatever conducts electricity is subject to gravitational attraction, jointly entail (3) All

metals are subject to gravitational attraction, but (1) and (2) certainly do not explain (3).

28 This is perhaps the occasion to introduce a minor modification both to (4″) and (4′). The points on the chain – the material points in the case of (4″) and the psychological points in the case of (4′) – must be the first points at which the chains have become permanently social-fact-free, as one goes backwards along them. Consider this explanatory chain: $m_1 \rightarrow p_1 \rightarrow s_1$. This chain, let us suppose, is social-fact-free to the left of m_1. (4″) and (4′) are meant to be alternatives, but the chain is consistent with both as stated, unless one adds the qualification about *first* points. Presumably, the chain should count as meeting the requirements of (4′), since methodological individualists have never intended to rule out the possibility that, in their turn, psychological facts might receive physiological explanations. With the qualification about *first* points, the chain above would be evidence for methodological individualism and not for methodological materialism.

First appendix to Chapter 4

1 K.R. Popper, *The Open Society and Its Enemies*, vol. 2, London, Routledge & Kegan Paul, 1969, p. 98.
2 *Ibid.*, p. 96.
3 *Ibid.*, pp. 96-7.
4 K.R. Popper, *The Open Society and Its Enemies*, vol. 1, London, Routledge & Kegan Paul, 1969, p. 315, fn. 63.
5 J.W.N. Watkins, 'Ideal types and historical explanation', reprinted in J. O'Neill (ed.), *Modes of Individualism and Collectivism*, London, Heinemann, 1973, p. 149.

Second appendix to Chapter 4

1 Philip Pettit, *Judging Justice*, London, Routledge & Kegan Paul, 1980, p. 63.

Name Index

Achinstein, P., 134
Armstrong, D.M., 2, 42, 72-3, 92, 98

Brodbeck, M., 185, fn. 14.
Burge, T., 65

Chisholm, R., 59-60, 61-5
Currie, G., 44

Danto, A., 45
Davidson, D., 134
Donnellan, K., 33-4
Dray, W., 146, 148-9
Dretske, F., 184, fn. 7.

Garfinkel, A., 106, 140-2

Hart, H.L.A., 21, 117
Hempel, C., 135, 146-7, 171
Hume, D., 11-12

Keynes, J.M., 126-7, 153
Kim, J., 94

Lesnoff, M., 16, 22
Lukes, S., 128-30

Macdonald, G., 45, 49, 55, 150-1,
    153, 162, 167
McGinn, C., 94-6
Mandelbaum, M., 2
Marx, K. 117
Mellor, D.H., 41, 144, 151, 153-4,
162, 167, 169
Miller, R., 163-4

Oppenheim, P., 45, 135

Pap, A., 32-3
Papineau, D., 29, 30, 43
Pettit, P., 31, 33, 34, 38, 45, 49, 55,
    150-1, 153, 162, 167, 177-9
Plantinga, A., 59-60
Popper, K.R., 154-5, 173-6
Putnam, H., 45, 94-103

Quine, W.V.O., 10
Quinton, A., 2, 4, 12, 13, 45, 49, 110

Rescher, N., 58, 68, 70
Russell, B., 13

Scriven, M., 146
Shwayder, D.S., 113, 116-17
Strawson, P., 76, 182 fn. 16

Unger, P., 33

van Fraassen, B., 144-5

Watkins, J.W.N., 1, 13, 126-7,
    150-1, 153, 163-4, 165, 167, 175
Weber, M., 9
Wiggins, D., 73, 76
Wright, C., 33-4

Subject Index

abstract objects, 37-8, 58, 71-2, 166-7
aggregates, 15-19, 65-7, 68, 73
alternative realisations, 91-105
ascending reason-relations, 112
asymmetry, 157

circularity, 6-8, 121-5

descending reason-relations, 113
disjunctive properties, 92, 98

elimination, 11-12, 42; *see also* reduction
explanandum, 134-5
explanans, 134-5
explanans-entity, 134-5
explanation, 142-50
explanation, object of, 134-5, 140-2
explanatory ancestor, 138, 156
explanatory chain, 138-9, 155-72
explanatory descendent, 138
explanatory priority, 131-2, 161-2
explanatory tree, 138-9
extensional equivalence, 43, 92-4

fact, 136; contrastive facts, 140-2; general facts, 137; particular facts, 137; social facts, 40, 139-40; universal facts, 137-8, 160-1
fetishism, 117

general belief, 33, 39
group, 19-23, 55-6, 75-6

holism: metaphysical v. methodological, 1, 131; p-holism v. e-holism, 3-4, 83, 88-91

hological essentialism, 59-61

ideal types, 9
identity criteria, 44
illuminating identities v. Reductive identities, 23-4, 36
indiscernibility of identicals, 56-9
individualism; metaphysical v. methodological, 1, 9, 131; p-individualism v. e-individualism, 3-4, 83, 88-91

laws, 160-1

material object, 73, 74, 80, 86-8
material property, 83-4, 86-8
materialism, 171-2; reductive v. eliminative, 11-12
membership relation, 47, 80-1
mental property, 83-4, 86-8, 153-4
mereological essentialism, 59-63
mereology, 45-8, 56-9
methodological materialism, 150-72
minds, 49-50, 81-2, 86-8, 115

nested systems, 109-17
nomologicity, 93-4, 99-102

objects v. properties, 3

perceptual salience, 177-9
phenomenalism, 2, 6, 28, 103, 168-9
physical, *see* material
psychological, 162-3
psychologism, 154-5, 173-5

rational explanation, 148-9

reduction of theories, 2, 46
reductive identification, 5-8, 42-4,
    91-4, 118-21
relationality, 26-9, 116
rules, 21, 117

sets, 15-19
singular belief, 32-8
social action, 121-3, 129-30
social property, 83, 86-8, 105-17,
    153-4; variable v. non-variable,
    119-21; weakly v. strongly, 121-7,
    128-30

social substance, 8-9
society, 54-5
space, 58, 74, 75
spatial locatability, 14, 50-2, 53-4,
    72-4, 75-6

transitivity: of the explanation
    relation, 149-50, 157; of the
    membership relation, 69, 78-9; of
    the part relation, 69-71
Turing Machines, 96-7